The *V*ICTORIOUS *C*HURCH
of the End Time

The Victorious Church of the End Time

the 21st century believer
and the next move of God

GRACE EMERALD UDOKANG

Copyright © 2011— Grace Emerald Udokang

All rights reserved. Pursuant to the Berne Convention. This book may not be copied or reprinted for commercial gain or profit. The use of short quotations or occasional page copying for personal or group study is permitted and encouraged. Permission will be granted upon request. Unless otherwise identified, Scripture quotations are taken from the New King James Version. Copyright © 1982 by Thomas Nelson, Inc. Used by permission. All rights reserved.

Please note that Destiny Image Europe's publishing style capitalizes certain pronouns in Scripture that refer to the Father, Son, and Holy Spirit, and may differ from some Bible publishers' styles. Take note that the name satan and related names are not capitalized. We choose not to acknowledge him, even to the point of violating grammatical rules.

DESTINY IMAGE™ EUROPE srl
Via Maiella, 1
66020 San Giovanni Teatino (Ch) – Italy

"Changing the world, one book at a time."

This book and all other Destiny Image™ Europe books are available at Christian bookstores and distributors worldwide.

To order products, or for any other correspondence:

DESTINY IMAGE™ EUROPE srl
Via della Scafa 29/14
65013 Città Sant'Angelo (Pe), Italy
Tel. +39 085 4716623 - +39 085 8670146
Fax +39 085 9090113
Email: info@eurodestinyimage.com
Or reach us on the Internet: www.eurodestinyimage.com

ISBN 13: 978-88-96727-27-0
ISBN 13 Ebook: 978-88-89127-58-4

For Worldwide Distribution, Printed in the U.S.A.
1 2 3 4 5 6 7 / 15 14 13 12 11

Acknowledgments

I thank God who has kept me alive for such a time as this and enabled me to be active in ministry.

I acknowledge the support of many people God has placed in my path to be of extraordinary blessing to my life and ministry.

I want to acknowledge the contributions of the entire congregation of Green Pastures Christian Center, who God has used to train me in spiritual disciplines and warfare.

My husband and friend, Engr. Kufre Udokang, my children, Ann, Darlingmoore, Stephen, Truth, Andrew, and Divine.

My family members, whose support and prayers have helped me in no small measure.

My mum, whose heart is full of goodness and prayers for my success.

I want to express as well my gratitude to all my staff past and present. Your commitments, dedication, and love have enabled me to do this work with minimal stress. My secretary—Blessing, God brought you at a time like this; thank you for being patient and considerate.

God bless and reward you all.

Endorsement

Pastor Grace has re-echoed the voice of the Spirit of God in a very simple but insightful presentation of present-moment truth about the state of the Church.

The present-day Church is still God's battle ax to subdue kingdoms and nations for our God. "The duller the ax, the harder the work." As it is for the ax, so it is for the Church.

This book is full of insight and wisdom on how to restore the cutting edge of the twenty-first century Church.

Pastor Ose Imiemohon
The Brook Church
Calabar, Nigeria

Contents

Chapter 1	The Twenty-first Century Church and the Next Move of God	13
Chapter 2	The Challenges of the Present Church	23
Chapter 3	Overcoming the Grasshopper Mentality and Dealing With the Giants	35
Chapter 4	The Old Testament Patterns: David	45
Chapter 5	David's Men: Ordinary Men Called to a New Destiny	67
Chapter 6	Nehemiah: The Passion for Revival	99
Chapter 7	Esther: Dying to Self: A Key to Breaking Ground for Victory	109
Chapter 8	Joshua: A Warrior With a Divine Vision	119
Chapter 9	Lessons for the Twenty-first Century Church	145
	Epilogue	149

Chapter 1

The Twenty-first Century Church and the Next Move of God

The Twenty-first Century Church and the Next Move of God

The Church is the ground, the pillar of truth, and the organ that God has kept on the earth to bring about His purposes. It is a body of believers called out from the world and its systems to display the power and the glorious excellence of God. This is not to say that the purposes of God are only worked out by the Church, as that would be too much limitation for a limitless God.

> But if I am delayed, I write so that you may know how you ought to conduct yourself in the house of God, which is the church of the living God, the pillar and ground of the truth (1 Timothy 3:15).

The whole world is working out God's purposes daily, but God works it out through the power generated by the Church through prayers. She is the engine room that generates the power needed to save the world and its systems. The revelations of God and His attributes were and are still committed to the Church, and until the Church finally shows the world through her manifestations of power and glory that true picture of God, the world and the systems cannot be delivered from the bondage of corruption and decay. The whole creation up until now is travailing in pain to experience the redemption that will come as a result of the manifestation of the sons of God.

For I consider that the sufferings of this present time are not worthy to be compared with the glory which shall be revealed in us. For the earnest expectation of the creation eagerly waits for the revealing of the sons of God. For the creation was subjected to futility, not willingly, but because of Him who subjected it in hope; because the creation itself also will be delivered from the bondage of corruption into the glorious liberty of the children of God. For we know that the whole creation groans and labors with birth pangs together until now. Not only that, but we also who have the first fruits of the Spirit, even we ourselves groan within ourselves, eagerly waiting for the adoption, the redemption of our body (Romans 8:18-23).

Arming the Saints

There is to my mind a misplacement of priorities by the vast majority of the leadership of the present Church, meaning those called into the five-fold ministry, whose primary assignment is to equip the saints so they can do the work of the ministry. Undue emphasis is placed on materialism and the pursuit of things in the name of teaching prosperity, to the detriment of character formation and Christ-likeness.

It is not uncommon to find in many religious circles pastors just interested in how much money individual members can bring, even if their lifestyles do not exemplify Christ in truth, honesty, integrity, and hard work.

While pursuing the building of adequate buildings or auditoriums is important, the primary focus of the Lord is the well-being of the souls of the people. Now cathedral building is an agenda pursued by present leadership instead of capacity building. In the mind of God, people are His prime focus. It is people, people, people. Whatever else the leadership is building today will not pass the mark with God unless it is directed to building up the people, indeed, the Body.

We all in the present leadership need to watch that we do not buy into the psychology of a needy Church with itching ears, helping the people to remain needy. And so, week in, week out, the people come with itching ears to hear what they need, we provide their needs by some supernatural manifestations, and the cycle continues, almost in perpetuity. This is an error. We need to strive both to meet the needs of the believers related to the daily struggles of life and also to focus on feeding them to come to the fullness of Christ so they can do the work of the ministry and fulfill their destinies. This is not to say that the needs of the people must be ignored, but to major on just fixing needs will keep the Church as spiritual babies and the entire Body will suffer.

> *And He Himself gave some to be apostles, some prophets, some evangelists, and some pastors and teachers, for the equipping of the saints for the work of ministry, for the edifying of the body of Christ, till we all come to the unity of the faith and of the knowledge of the Son of God, to a perfect man, to the measure of the stature of the fullness of Christ* (Ephesians 4:11-13).

Leadership has been given to equip the people so they can in turn do the work of the ministry, and as that work is done the whole Body will be edified. That indeed is the whole essence of having the apostles, prophets, pastors, teachers, and evangelists.

This present Church is the Church with the ultimate weapon of warfare that will tear the veil and the covering cast over all the nations of the earth to cover the earth with God's glory as the water covers the sea.

All those with prophetic sights have and are still declaring that there is a move of God coming upon the earth, which will make Pentecost seem like child's play.

There is a present move of God on the earth, and that move will finally birth the return of Jesus. The heavens have been configured to retain Christ until certain conditions on the earth are fulfilled.

> *Repent therefore and be converted, that your sins may be blotted out, so that times of refreshing may come from the presence of the Lord, and that He may send Jesus Christ, who was preached to you before, whom heaven must receive until the times of restoration of all things, which God has spoken by the mouth of all His holy prophets since the world began* (Acts 3:19-21).

There is an amount of spiritual power and strength needed to counter the abounding evil in the atmosphere of the earth and facilitate the release of Christ. That power has to be generated by the Church.

> *And behold, there was a man in Jerusalem whose name was Simeon, and this man was just and devout, waiting for the Consolation of Israel, and the Holy Spirit was upon him. And it had been revealed to him by the Holy Spirit that he would not see death before he had seen the Lord's Christ* (Luke 2:25-26).

> *Now there was one, Anna, a prophetess, the daughter of Phanuel, of the tribe of Asher. She was of a great age, and had lived with a husband seven years from her virginity* (Luke 2:36).

Just as it was in Jesus' first coming where God had to raise up Simeon and Anna as part of an intercessory team to birth Christ in the flesh and they defied death to see the promise, so shall it be in this dispensation. Men and women will be strategically positioned in the Body of Christ and indeed are now positioned. These will be the company whose intercessions will provide the corporate spiritual force and power needed to get the heavens to release the Messiah again.

BIRTHING OF THE SONS OF GOD

I would like to call that move the "Birthing of the Sons of God." All through time and everything God does, He always starts in a seed form, empowering the seed to bring forth after its kind; so it is also with Christ Jesus. When Jesus came to the earth, He did not only come to reveal God but to show humanity how to represent God on the earth. He is the firstborn among many brothers.

> *For whom He foreknew, He also predestined to be conformed to the image of His Son, that He might be the firstborn among many brethren* (Romans 8:29).

Jesus also declared:

> *Most assuredly, I say to you, he who believes in Me, the works that I do he will do also; and greater works than these he will do, because I go to My Father* (John 14:12).

This next move of God calls for a total restructuring of the anatomical and physiological makeup of the Church we know today.

All through the ages, God's mind had always been to get a people on the earth who will bring about His intentions and execute them with accuracy and precision. He has always been looking for a man to spearhead these operations. But His ultimate desire is always to get a body of people. We can see the patterns in His choice of Abraham, Isaac, Jacob, Joseph, and Israel.

The present Church, that is the twenty-first century Church, is His ultimate instrument for the ultimate end of satan's rulership on the earth.

> *To the intent that now the manifold wisdom of God might be made known by the church to the principalities and powers in the heavenly places* (Ephesians 3:10).

This move of God has in its center the Zion Church. That is the Church that will form the catalytic mass to spread the glory. "Out of Zion, the perfection of beauty, God will shine forth" (Ps. 50:2).

The whole Body of Christ as we know it today will not all be involved initially. There is a church within the Church. This is the "Man Child" company or Esther Company or a Joshua generation.

These are they who have washed their garments clean and are following the Lamb wherever He goes. Their mentality is that of pilgrims on the earth, and "They go from strength to strength; each one appears before God in Zion" (Ps. 84:7).

The present move is what will cause the heavens to release Christ in the Church first before He comes for the Church. With all that is happening in the world today, the Church stands in a very strategic position to change the face of the earth by the release of a brand-new set of saints. A people strong and mighty, a fire devouring before them and behind them utter desolation.

> *A day of darkness and gloominess, a day of clouds and thick darkness, like the morning clouds spread over the mountains. A people come, great and strong, the like of whom has never been; nor will there ever be any such after them, even for many successive generations. A fire devours before them, and behind them a flame burns; the land is like the Garden of Eden before them, and behind them a desolate wilderness; surely nothing shall escape them* (Joel 2:2-3).

Just as there were challenges in the Church of the first century, so also challenges abound now but in a different and more intensified dimension. This present Church must not only tackle these challenges for its survival, but must present a way for the world to escape.

Points to Ponder

1. In the mind of God, people are His prime focus. It is people, people, people.
2. This present Church is the Church with the ultimate weapon of warfare that will tear the veil and the covering cast over all the nations of the earth to cover the earth with God's glory as the water covers the sea.

3. God always starts in a seed form, empowering the seed to bring forth after its kind.
4. With all that is happening in the world today, the Church stands in a very strategic position to change the face of the earth by the release of a brand-new set of saints.

Chapter 2

The Challenges of the Present Church

The Challenges of the Present Church

I will define the Church as a collection of the redeemed (believers) submitted to the Redeemer and to each other in the fear or reverence of God. Each believer is also an individual church.

The early Church demonstrated this fully when they separated themselves as a called-out people. Our separation today should not have a monastic approach, but it should be in our mentalities and the values that shape them. The Church that will shape and change the systems of the world cannot be seen flirting with those systems. It is my belief that no one can bring a lasting change to any system of which he is part.

For this change to come, the Church has to first understand the nature of the mandate she has received from God and the urgency of that commission. There is urgency in the mind of God for the execution of the mandate.

Spiritual Values

From eternity, God had put all things in place, and there is nothing that is out of order in His universe that He made. There is an orderly arrangement of His plans and purposes, and not even the chaotic nature of humanity can derail His intents and purposes. Eternity is in the heart of every person, and God put it there. God is a Spirit, and so the first nature of anything He does is spiritual.

Man is a spirit, but he possesses a soul and lives in a body. The body of man gives him access and contact with the material world, but essentially man's source of all things is derived from the spirit. God has had everything figured out since Adam, including how He was going to eventually redeem His creation from corruption.

In this present dispensation, He ordained that the Church should be the instrument through which He will achieve that. All through His dealings, He had always brought a man out of a nation to be a leader through whom He can work to deliver the nation. We see that in His choices of people like Abraham, Joseph, Moses, David, and many others. His intent always is the salvation of a people.

The Scriptures clearly state that in the last days men shall be excessively wicked, and troubles will abound on the earth as a result of abounding evil (see 2 Tim. 3:1-9).

We are indeed living in the last of the last days, and God is looking for a body of people to bring forth His eternal purposes.

This group of people must have certain values and belief systems to qualify for the outpouring of God's purposes in and through them. They must possess a new paradigm and have the ability and capacity to access and download heavenly treasures and resources for humanity.

They must be discerning of the times and the seasons of God's dealings on the earth, like the Sons of Issachar. They must migrate to the new positions in the spirit.

> *Of the sons of Issachar who had understanding of the times, to know what Israel ought to do, their chiefs were two hundred; and all their brethren were at their command* (1 Chronicles 12:32).

There is an emergence of a new season of God on the earth; this season demands strict adherence to instructions particularly on the part of the leadership—accountability, responsibility, faithfulness, and capacity to hear and follow God. This is not the time to take God for granted.

The ultimate demand is the building of character and integrity. The deeper one goes in repentance now, the more fruit one is able to bear. This season cannot be accessed by casual seekers of God; only the diligent can see the glory of this season. This is the season of divine selection.

In the Scriptures, we see a pattern of the caliber of men and women who God raised up in their generations to carry out His divine purposes on the earth. Also in this dispensation, God is raising up His elite forces who will possess the ability to deal the final blow to the enemy and his hordes. These people will defeat the last enemy and wear immortality as a garment over their mortal bodies.

"For this corruptible must put on incorruption, and this mortal must put on immortality" (1 Cor. 15:53). For this to happen they must dispossess their minds of the grasshopper mentality, deal decisively with the giants in the land of their possession, and only then can the final battle against satan and his cohorts be won.

Present-Day Darkness

The present Church is faced with the challenge of having to present the love of God to a loveless generation. The world, as we are well aware, is increasingly advancing toward a catastrophic end. People have become increasingly wicked and insensitive.

> *But know this, that in the last days perilous times will come: for men will be lovers of themselves, lovers of money, boasters, proud, blasphemers, disobedient to parents, unthankful, unholy, unloving, unforgiving, slanderers, without self-control, brutal, despisers of good, traitors, headstrong, haughty, lovers*

of pleasure rather than lovers of God, having a form of godliness but denying its power. And from such people turn away! For of this sort are those who creep into households and make captives of gullible women loaded down with sins, led away by various lusts, always learning and never able to come to the knowledge of the truth (2 Timothy 3:1-7).

In spite of the fact that there is so much knowledge on the earth today, people are still trying to grasp the truth of God's Word.

But you, Daniel, shut up the words, and seal the book until the time of the end; many shall run to and fro, and knowledge shall increase (Daniel 12:4).

The past one hundred years have produced technological breakthroughs that the whole of history put together has never witnessed—the Internet, the satellite, cell phones, and diverse medical and scientific inventions. Today we can fly across the oceans at a speed that was unthinkable decades ago.

My grandfather—who left about thirty years ago—would be dazed if he arrived in the world today to see how technology has evolved and is affecting every sphere of human existence. He would not know what to do with the 3D HDTVs (three dimensional high definition televisions) or any of the gadgets we have today. He'd probably look at my Blackberry in awe. How is it possible to get instant mail and pictures sent thousands of miles away in a matter of seconds?

All this is to illustrate how far people have gone in developing and enhancing our standards of living. Life is a lot easier. My microwave will get my food done in a matter of minutes. No more firewood, charcoal pots, etc. But, sad to say, the more humankind continues to advance technologically, the more they are losing touch with the Creator. And right now perversion is the order of the world—men marrying men, women and men changing sexes, ministers paying prostitutes, and mass murderers getting more hardened until Hitler's wickedness loses its prime position in comparison. Religious leaders order mass executions in the name of serving God. New weapons of mass destruction and seduction abound. Ravaging diseases that have defied medical science are still springing up.

When Noah's world was wiped out, it never witnessed the enormity witnessed in the world today. I think Sodom and Gomorrah are wondering what God is doing now, when they were destroyed for less. All this is to attest to the fact that we are in the last of the last days, and because the Church is on the earth and praying, the hand of the enemy is somewhat restrained. The question now is, "For how long?"

"And because lawlessness will abound, the love of many will grow cold" (Matt. 24:12). The Church too is now increasingly losing its cutting edge because of abounding compromise. She is trying to compete with the world instead of *completing* the world. The world is lacking in godliness and righteousness, and the Church should be showing the world how to live and not die. All this is happening because of the abounding iniquity in the atmosphere. The Church has to combat this menace or find herself in compromising stands at all times.

In the days of Jesus, while He was in the flesh, the Bible records:

> *Who, in the days of His flesh, when He had offered up prayers and supplications, with vehement cries and tears to Him who was able to save Him from death, and was heard because of His godly fear* (Hebrews 5:7).

He was delivered, heard, and kept from the evil of His environment because He put certain laws of God into action—the law of the spirit of life. It is clear in the Scriptures that there are two laws operating in the universe:

1. The law of sin and death
2. The law of the spirit of life in Christ

There is therefore now no condemnation to those who are in Christ Jesus, who do not walk according to the flesh, but according to the Spirit. For the law of the Spirit of life in Christ Jesus has made me free from the law of sin and death (Romans 8:1-2).

If the law of sin and death is to have no effect on the Church, then there must be a deliberate and diligent work of the Spirit to counter it. In other words, the law of life must be enforced, and the only way to do that is basically through intercessions.

The Need for Intercessors

I think this is the real problem of the present Church. Intercession has been set aside for a select few. The Body of Christ will enjoy every other thing except to fall on its face before God in repentance and prayer. As a pastor, I have seen that the meetings most people want to miss in church are the prayer meetings. The appetites for prayer have and still are dwindling. People are no longer interested in seeking God for God's sake, but they seek Him for things and in so doing are missing out on the benefits of true fellowship, obedience, faith, and growth. The Church now wants to be like the world, and the world is crying to know God.

The present Church is facing the challenge of excessive materialism. A man's life is now increasingly measured by the things he possesses. The Church has joined the rat race.

People are no longer judged by the content of their character but by the contents of their bank account and material possessions. Judging external appearances has replaced the true judgments of the hearts and the intents of the same. Pastors are celebrating the Achans of this generation instead of rebuking, correcting, and judging them as the laws of God demand. The focus is no longer on the weightier matters of the law—faith, judgment, and mercy.

Even though we are living in a material world, the issues that affect humanity can never be solved with acquisition of more and more. Poverty is a spiritual disease that can affect even those with material things. Poverty is not only the absence of money, but the absence of spiritual power to deal with the other issues in life that money cannot solve. Money cannot save a person from premature physical death if a demonic spirit is oppressing him in that respect.

This present Church needs to possess the power needed to challenge the demonic spirits that have been assigned by satan himself to devastate the earth. This requires a militant approach as opposed to the complacent and noncommittal attitude of many in the present Church.

True leadership and clear prophetic voices need to be reintroduced in the present Church. Men and women should arise to take their positions in the midst of the ongoing jamboree. They will be a people who have a clearly defined mandate from God to deal with the ills of the present formation of the Church.

The pastors should speedily turn the focus of people from things to God. Integrity should be taught once more, for only integrity will deliver the upright person. Idolatry should be called what it is. When people pursue things and keep God in second place, they should be called who they are—idol worshipers.

Pampering spirits should be thrown out of the Church. If people are willing to do right and follow God, they should be encouraged. If iniquity is still too attractive to them, they should be made to choose who they will serve. Leadership needs to be rid of hypocrisy and duplicity.

The Church should never be a breeding place for religious spirits. God abhors religions. I tell people that God is not interested in an outward show that is bereft of inward strength. The way to display the manifold wisdom of God to principalities and powers is the way of force, and a religious church cannot enforce any decrees. It is too weak and compromised to be of any good to the Kingdom of God.

This to my mind is a heavy challenge. With man it may seem impossible, but with God all things are possible. God will surely have a people in the midst of the chaos.

CLEAR-SIGHTED

The Church lacks clarity of sight. A Church without accurate sight can never experience the fullness of the omnipotence of God. Accurate sight is lacking in the Church because of wrong focus. Whatever you pay attention to is what will give you direction.

Jesus said:

> *The lamp of the body is the eye. If therefore your eye is good, your whole body will be full of light. But if your eye is bad, your whole body will be full of darkness. If therefore the light that is in you is darkness, how great is that darkness! No one can serve two masters; for either he will hate the one and love the other, or else he will be loyal to the one and despise the other. You cannot serve God and mammon* (Matthew 6:22-24).

When the hearts of the church leaders are truly set to know God and fulfill His purposes, only then shall the people be instructed in the ways of God. The question every church leader should ask himself is this: "Whose kingdom am I building, God's or self's?" When they can truly and reverently answer this question, only then can they expect to do differently than they are presently doing.

There is a dearth of accurate leadership and it comes from inaccurate sight. Inaccurate sight caused Israel to see themselves as grasshoppers and their enemies as giants.

Until there is an accurate representation of God's view to the world, gross darkness will cover the people and there will be no hope for the world or the Church. This is a serious challenge, and the Zion Church will have to pray so the whole Body of Christ will be full of light.

This is the time to be among the five wise virgins who took their lamps out and also had extra oil. The Church is operating on residual oil, and there is a cry that the Bridegroom is coming. The only thing that can help us now is the extra oil in our earthen vessels. We can safely deduce from the story of the ten virgins that half of the present church formation may not see God unless they change.

The five foolish virgins who came back later were told, "I never knew you." This to my mind is a tragedy.

Points to Ponder

1. The present Church needs leadership with accurate sight who will be accountable, responsible, faithful, and have the capacity to hear and follow God.
2. Integrity and character of God must be emphasized above materialism.
3. The laws of the spirit of life in Christ must be activated by the Church.
4. The leaders will have to live by example for the flock to follow.
5. Leaders should never expect followers to get to where they themselves have not attained, spiritually speaking.
6. God is changing all things, and leaders should embrace God's mind before they can affect their congregation.

Chapter 3

Overcoming the Grasshopper Mentality and Dealing With the Giants

Overcoming the Grasshopper Mentality and Dealing With the Giants

The Bible records that when Moses sent the spies out they came back reporting that there were giants in the land. They reported the facts of what they saw, but in the light of the Word of God there is a difference between facts and truth.

> And the Lord spoke to Moses saying "Send men to spy out the land of Canaan, which I am giving to the children of Israel; from each tribe of their fathers you shall send a man, every one a leader among them" (Numbers 13:1-2).

What they saw and reported were the facts of the situation, but when they refused to go in because of the facts then they rendered the truth null and void. The truth was that the land was theirs, but they limited God by choosing to act on the facts of their situation. What you do or do not do in any situation is what actually determines the efficacy of the Word of God in your own experience. In other words, God needs your faith and cooperation to bring His truth to pass in your situation.

THE GIANTS

The giants were the result of the union between the "Sons of God"—fallen angels—and the daughters of men. The giants came into existence after Noah's flood, and they occupied the land of Canaan in the time of Abraham. The aim of the fallen angels who cohabited with the daughters of men was to corrupt the human race and thereby make it impossible for the pure seed of the woman to come as predicted.

So the giants were in the land when God promised to give it to Abraham. To the present-day people of God, giants represent situations that have been manipulated and controlled by demonic forces to bring intimidation, fear, and ultimately death to the purpose or vision of the believer. In some cases, these forces try to bring about the actual death of the believer.

They represent imposing circumstances that defy the natural ability of anyone to cope with. They represent situations that science and nature have no answer for. Situations that seem impossible. Situations that seek to defy every form of progress in the life of an individual.

In summary, they present difficult situations that defy your strength, resources, or tact. Giants are imposing, and they naturally bring fear and helplessness wherever their voices trumpet. They loom larger than life and dare you to defy them.

Perhaps you have had situations in your life that were life-threatening or some that just threatened your progress. Have you ever been presented with a situation that medical science has no answer for? Have you been told that you are doomed to live and die in mediocrity and poverty? Adversity is played out before you almost in perpetuity. If hopelessness and helplessness stare at you, then obviously you are facing giants.

You see, it's possible to go through life and allow adverse circumstances to steer your destiny into the path of destruction and mediocrity. You can live and die without an epitaph on your tombstone, or even without a tombstone, because everyone around you, including yourself, has been held bound by lack and want.

If you have been held back, held down, and stopped from advancing in life, then you urgently need to learn the act of spiritual warfare and possess every inch of what God has given you.

In Luke 13, the woman in the synagogue represents believers who seem to be making progress but aren't. She could not straighten up or even look up. The Bible records she was bent forward. This is a position that appears progressive—bent forward like a runner. But, like running on a treadmill, it's really just running around and going nowhere.

The enemy has a way of deluding us to believe that progress is just around the corner. Let me say this, until you remove the enemy from your circumstances you can die being deluded. I often watch people circle around in life, not confronting the issues, and years come and go, passing them by in the same position.

The Bible records in First Samuel 17 that Goliath appeared before the army of Israel day and night for 40 days, and as long as there was no man to challenge and confront him, Israel would have stayed there, just transfixed and awed by that uncircumcised giant.

Until a man came to confront him, no progress was made. Satan lives in eternity, and your life span of 70, 80, or even 100 years means absolutely nothing in comparison. He does not mind just keeping you in one position and watching you waste.

Satan's main reason for fighting you is not to make you poor or kill you, just for your sake. His purpose is to stop you from reaching and getting everything that your Creator designed you to be. If poverty is what can stop you, be sure he will use it. If having riches will stop you, be sure he will give you enough.

When Jesus came to the world, satan—knowing in advance His mission and purpose—came to offer Him the world and the glitz and glamour therein. Had Jesus bowed to that temptation, salvation for humanity would be lost. Jesus ultimately got the whole world, but there was a prescribed way—the way of the Cross. Any time the enemy presents the crown without the Cross, he is presenting another gospel, and another gospel is a direct route to the abortion of purpose. In order to access your goals and destiny, you must be willing to confront the giants. The greater your goals and destiny, the greater the force of evil you have to confront.

The Grasshoppers

So when Israel got to the land, they saw the giants and that was OK. God has never promised a storm-free life, but He said like eagles the storms will come to spur us unto greater heights.

What was wrong was their estimation of themselves. They saw themselves as grasshoppers, and that was a very dangerous posture to assume in the face of the gigantic issues that confronted them. In other words, they believed their physical sight and told God He lied to them.

Nothing insults the integrity of God as much as a lack of spiritual sight. Faith can never be fully expressed without insight into who God is and what He can do. To overcome the giants you must overcome the grasshopper mindset. The only defeat that can be permanent is that which comes from the mind of the man himself. As a person thinks, so it is.

The grasshopper mindset comes as a result of the intimidating fear that advertises the problems more than the Word of God. Any time a person sees his problem as a mountain and the Word of God as a mole hill, he automatically incapacitates God's ability to prove Himself.

No matter what you face, God has exalted His Word above all His names, and His Word will not return to Him void. If you refuse to believe Him, His Word will find a believing vessel to fulfill His desire.

God admonished His people in Isaiah:

> *Do not say, "A conspiracy," concerning all that this people call a conspiracy, nor be afraid of their threats, nor be*

troubled. The Lord of hosts, Him you shall hallow; let Him be your fear, and let Him be your dread (Isaiah 8:12-13).

Joshua and Caleb bore witness to that fact. They were with the rest of the people, but they chose to believe God in spite of the physical evidence.

The report you choose to believe is what can give you a resounding victory or defeat in your circumstances.

> *Now they departed and came back to Moses and Aaron and all the congregation of the children of Israel in the Wilderness of Paran, at Kadesh; they brought back word to them and to all the congregation, and showed them the fruit of the land. Then they told him, and said: "We went to the land where you sent us. It truly flows with milk and honey, and this is its fruit. Nevertheless the people who dwell in the land are strong; the cities are fortified and very large; moreover we saw the descendants of Anak there. The Amalekites dwell in the land of the South; the Hittites, the Jebusites, and the Amorites dwell in the mountains; and the Canaanites dwell by the sea and along the banks of the Jordan." Then Caleb quieted the people before Moses, and said, "Let us go up at once and take possession, for we are well able to overcome it." But the men who had gone up with him said, "We are not able to go up against the people, for they are stronger than we." And they gave the children of Israel a bad report of the land which they had spied out, saying, "The land through which we have gone as spies is a land that devours its inhabitants, and all the people whom we saw in it are men of great stature. There we saw the giants (the descendants of Anak came from the giants); and we were like grasshoppers in our own sight, and so we were in their sight" (Numbers 13:26-33).*

It is clear that the believer is going to be challenged by real situations and his physical wits and tact grossly tested, but God has not left us to ourselves. He said, "I will be with you even to the end of time."

The giants were deliberately allowed in the land so God could train His people in the art of warfare. God does not intend that we be defeated before the enemies, but that the enemies may see that He is with us.

To overcome the giants, believers should never compare the giants with themselves but should see the giants in the light of the omnipotent Jehovah. Our God must be bigger than our situations if we ever hope to overcome. Faith must be activated, for without it, it is impossible to please God.

In this present time, so many issues are daily defying human reasoning and comprehension, and so attention should be turned to the God who has an answer to every situation.

Sometimes it is easier to pray that situations that challenge us do not even come, but then we will be limited in the knowledge of God. How can we possibly know the power of His resurrection without the fellowship of His sufferings?

> *Yet indeed I also count all things loss for the excellence of the knowledge of Christ Jesus my Lord, for whom I have suffered the loss of all things, and count them as rubbish, that I may gain Christ and be found in Him, not having my own righteousness, which is from the law, but that which is through faith in Christ, the righteousness which is from God by faith; that I may know Him and the power of His resurrection, and the fellowship of His sufferings, being conformed to His death, if, by any means, I may attain to the resurrection from the dead (Philippians 3:8-11).*

Accurate understanding of the operations and the purposes of God will deliver this present Church from the grasshopper mentality.

For instance, when Israel left Egypt, God's intention was to train them in the wilderness and in so doing rid them of the slave mentality. His mind was to teach them dependency on Him, but limited knowledge of the mind of God and inability to express faith in God brought about their demise in the wilderness.

These things were written for our example; so declare the Scriptures:

> *Moreover, brethren, I do not want you to be unaware that all our fathers were under the cloud, all passed through the sea, all were baptized into Moses in the cloud and in the sea, all ate the same spiritual food, and all drank the same spiritual drink. For they drank of that spiritual Rock that followed them, and that Rock was Christ. But with most of them God was not well pleased, for their bodies were scattered in the wilderness. Now these things became our examples, to the intent that we should not lust after evil things as they also lusted. And do not become idolaters as were some of them. As it is written, "The people sat down to eat and drink, and rose up to play." Nor let us commit sexual immorality, as some of them did, and in one day twenty-three thousand fell; nor let us tempt Christ, as some of them also tempted, and were destroyed by serpents; nor complain, as some of them also complained, and were destroyed by the destroyer. Now all these things happened to them as examples, and they were written for our admonition, upon whom the ends of the ages have come* (1 Corinthians 10:1-11).

This present Church must be determined more than ever to know God more accurately, love Him more dearly, and serve Him passionately. Then we can overcome the giants in our generation, because we will have known Him as we are known.

Our Faith

The great men and women of old faced many giants and tact-defying circumstances, but in all these they obtained a good report that they overcame. The Book of Hebrews in the eleventh chapter is full of the exploits of faith.

We in this generation must possess the kind of faith that God had when He called forth order in a chaotic universe. The issues that seek to defy the Word of God in our lives must be challenged with the same Word they seek to nullify. This is the victory that overcomes the world—*our faith*.

Let us examine those attributes and patterns in the lives of the fathers of our faith and learn the valuable lessons from their lives.

We can be true overcomers even in the midst of a chaotic world and satanic rage. In the song, "A Mighty Fortress Is Our God," Martin Luther wrote, "Though this world with devils filled may threaten to undo us, we will not fear for God has willed His truth to triumph through us." With this mindset, let God be true and every devil a liar. Every giant will be destroyed out of our land of inheritance.

The boundary lines are indeed fallen to us in pleasant places, and this generation has a goodly heritage (see Ps. 16:6).

Points to Ponder

1. Believe the Word above your circumstances.
2. Refuse to be intimidated by the things you see.
3. Know that God is with you always to fight and overcome for you.
4. Increase your faith. Faith is the victory that overcomes the world.
5. Never see yourself in the light of how you perceive the enemies. You are who and what God says you are regardless of physical circumstances.

Chapter 4

The Old Testament Patterns: David

The Old Testament Patterns: David

We are living in a time when God will have to let go of the religious church that has no answer for the giants. Our giants are like those that gathered Israel into a valley of compromise, intimidation, fear, and indecision. The Bible records that there was war between Israel and the Philistines, and Saul was the king of Israel at that time.

THE CHURCH WITHOUT POWER

Now the Philistines gathered their armies together to battle, and were gathered together at Sochoh, which belongs to Judah; they encamped between Sochoh and Azekah, in Ephes Dammim. And Saul and the men of Israel were gathered together, and they encamped in the Valley of Elah, and drew up in battle array against the Philistines (1 Samuel 17:1-2).

Israel gathered in the valley of Sochoh, but for 40 days they had no answer for the giant who challenged them. Saul represents the religious church—a church with minimal or no relationship with their Maker. They go through the motions and lack the power. Saul also represents the selective obedient leaders who tell the church just part of the Gospel and not the full Gospel because they also cannot endure the full length of God's dealings.

> Samuel also said to Saul, "The Lord sent me to anoint you king over His people, over Israel. Now therefore, heed the voice of the words of the Lord. Thus says the Lord of hosts: 'I will punish Amalek for what he did to Israel, how he ambushed him on the way when he came up from Egypt. Now go and attack Amalek, and utterly destroy all that they have, and do not spare them. But kill both man and woman, infant and nursing child, ox and sheep, camel and donkey'" (1 Samuel 15:1-3).

Saul kept back some things in pretext to sacrifice to God. What sacrifice does God require but a broken and contrite spirit? What offering other than our burnt flesh? When we "kill" some things in us and refuse to deal with some, then we will become the church that is nothing but a dead lion, lacking power to deal with the giants that challenge us daily.

The Church of Jesus Christ is the instrument for the destruction of satan and his cohorts, but alas! The ax head has fallen. In other words, the cutting edge is gone; the Church has become a toothless bulldog.

> But as one was cutting down a tree, the iron ax head fell into the water; and he cried out and said, "Alas, master! For it was borrowed" (2 Kings 6:5).

The Church has lost her cutting edge. The Philistine giant is on rampage, and what can we say? For we have sinned. I say this under a powerful unction of the Holy Ghost:

> The time has come, and now is that time. God is releasing the unknown servants who have been faithful, truthful, and fruitful in their callings and have gone through the disciplines and trainings from the bears and the lions, and right now they have been sent on an errand by the Father to the camp where they will hear the challenge of Goliath and

make themselves available so the Father can be glorified. Their faith will be tried and tested that it might be seen by all that they possess the overcoming faith. Yes, those whose names and genealogies are not known; yes, those whose credentials amount to nothing, for they have none; yes, even those who had just few helpless sheep but have been faithful; yes, they are coming out to give the Church an answer for Goliath, that it may be known that God is not only in them, with them, but He is in His Church.

THE CONFRONTATION OF A SHEPHERD BOY

David arrived at the scene in First Samuel 17 and heard the challenge. He moved around to find out what would be done for the man who killed Goliath. But his elder brother got angry.

Now Eliab his oldest brother heard when he spoke to the men; and Eliab's anger was aroused against David, and he said, "Why did you come down here? And with whom have you left those few sheep in the wilderness? I know your pride and the insolence of your heart, for you have come down to see the battle" (1 Samuel 17:28).

There are people in the church who will get angry at others who just got born again and are ready to use their faith in God to deal with Goliath. Let him who is angry be angry still. Paul the apostle was born again without even seeing Jesus in the flesh, and he became a mighty apostle and God used him to write about two-thirds of the New Testament Scriptures.

It is not how long you have been around God and church but how faithful and diligent you have been that counts. God is releasing right now eleventh-hour laborers, so let our elder brothers grow up in their faith. There is no status quo in God, and He is not partial in the dispensing of His resources. The plowman will overtake the reaper; we are in that season.

> *"Behold, the days are coming," says the Lord, "When the plowman shall overtake the reaper, and the treader of grapes him who sows seed; the mountains shall drip with sweet wine, and all the hills shall flow with it"* (Amos 9:13).

David refused to be distracted by his brother's envy-ridden comments, but pressed on until he was brought to King Saul. Hear what he said: "I will go and kill the uncircumcised Philistine, and it will be known that there is a God in Israel."

> *Then David said to Saul, "Let no man's heart fail because of him; your servant will go and fight with this Philistine"* (1 Samuel 17:32).

Saul, the religious leader, said, "Do not go; you are too young and inexperienced." I wonder how King Saul concluded David was inexperienced. In this present day, God's dealings with the faithful are highly internalized, and any attempt to judge such people from their external appearances amounts to a serious error in judgment.

David replied by narrating his experience with the bear and the lion and the God who helped him. Saul agreed, but on the condition that David wore his armor. An armor is a protective covering, and Saul's armor was fashioned like that of Goliath. What a shame that the Church is borrowing the principles of the world to fight for survival. God said clearly, "Not by might nor by power, but by My Spirit" (Zech. 4:6).

We see the Church using all kinds of unethical and unscriptural methods to achieve "success." I say "success" in quotes because there is good success and there is bad success. The prosperity of fools shall destroy them. When the church uses public relations personnel to sell the image of the church and advertise by the same means, the church has a problem. When we have to use deception and hypocrisy to generate wealth, then we have a problem. When we have to prophesy lies to get to people's bank accounts and hearts, then we have a serious problem. This happens when people do not tithe because they feel that the money is too much and they cannot trust the integrity of the pastors to judiciously and effectively disburse the same. These people may be "rich" but they are violating God and consequently lack true success. We know of instances where Pentecostal pastors have gone to witch doctors and the occult to seek power to grow their churches.

In other words, Saul said to David, "I have protective covering for you, but is according to the principles and doctrine of the Philistines; use it to succeed." Hey, wait a minute! Why did Saul not use it long before David came to the scene to challenge Goliath? Saul represents a kind of leadership that wants to limit your potentiality in God by presenting the principles of the world and not teaching correctly the uncompromised Word of the Lord because they lack the faith they profess. This is a leadership who has many questions and no personal answers, yet is not humble enough to learn from supposed "newcomers." A leadership that has failed in activating God's people to face their challenges squarely will fail the same way Saul failed. Imagine gathering the whole army of Israel and just hearing the taunts and defiance of Goliath with no answers. Oh, how the Church has been reduced to a mere audience by compromising leadership!

David, who was a man of wisdom, knew that if he wore Saul's armor he would entangle himself in it and would never be able to approach the war to conquer Goliath, so he declined.

> *David fastened his sword to his armor and tried to walk, for he had not tested them. And David said to Saul, "I cannot walk with these, for I have not tested them." So David took them off* (1 Samuel 17:39).

It is time for the Church to have clear perspective of her call and duty on the earth. If the Church cannot provide the answer to the numerous ills that are plaguing our world today, then the world is doomed. But God forbid! God has a remnant, like David, who will rise to the challenges of the Goliaths of this day and bring victory to humanity and glory to the Almighty. So David put off Saul's armor and picked what he had tested and proved.

Time to Go for the Kill

Then he took his staff in his hand; and he chose for himself five smooth stones from the brook, and put them in a shepherd's bag, in a pouch which he had, and his sling was in his hand. And he drew near to the Philistine (1 Samuel 17:40).

The believer is over-resourced by God to deal with any and every kind of challenge that life has to offer, but many times we allow the enemy to run riot around us because of lack of knowledge of the changeless omnipotence and faithfulness of God. Let me say here that God will not do a thing without man's cooperation. Until you cooperate with Him through faith, victory will be unrealized.

How many times have we limited God by lack of knowledge? "The children of Ephraim, being armed and carrying bows, turned back in the day of battle" (Ps. 78:9).

The Bible says clearly that, "...the people who know their God shall be strong, and carry out great exploits" (Dan. 11:32). This knowledge is not a superficial one, but a deep, tested, and proven experience of God's omnipotence and faithfulness. It comes through intimate experiences in the avenues of persecutions and afflictions. Many times God will allow us to face little challenges here and there, and at times we find ourselves compromising here and there, but in compromise one misses the very experience that God's hand of victory would have given us.

Compromise has always been used by the enemy to dull the potency of God's Word in us and deny us of experiential knowledge of His omnipotence and faithfulness. But David had experience with the bear and the lion and he said:

...The Lord, who delivered me from the paw of the lion and from the paw of the bear, He will deliver me from the hand of this Philistine (1 Samuel 17:37).

This is the statement of a man with experiential knowledge of God. Until you fully comprehend the God of yesterday, you will not know Him for today or tomorrow. Until you can tell of His faithfulness in times past, you have nothing to hold out against the enemy of today or even that of tomorrow. Knowledge of God is critical if we are to deal with giants in the land.

Physical Sight an Ally With Satan

In spiritual warfare one needs to go past what the physical sight and sense are relaying. David's choice of weapon was no match for those of Goliath. Here in lies the truth of God's Word, that, "The horse is prepared for the day of battle, but deliverance is of the Lord" (Prov. 21:31). Were David to go by physical sight and sense, then the things he saw and sensed told him, "You are no match." But he went past those and got hold of faith—even faith in the God who has promised and cannot fail, and all enemies will become His footstool. "The Lord said to my Lord, 'Sit at My right hand, till I make Your enemies Your footstool'" (Ps. 110:1).

Most times our problems loom larger than life itself; but when you match them with the strength of your God and your faith in Him, they just become shadows in the light of His presence. We need elevated sight to succeed.

The Bible says Jordan saw God and fled the sea also, and even Jericho fell, not because of what Israel did, because they did nothing but walked around (see Ps. 114:1-8 and Josh. 6). God's presence will cause every giant in your life to simply fade out. Don't deny your problems; don't run from them either; confront them with God's presence and every mountain will melt like wax. I guarantee you that no mountain can withstand His presence. Our problem is we don't have much of His presence with us.

Presence Is Cultivated Through Prayer

A prayerful Christian is a powerful Christian, because in a place of prayer there is always a divine exchange. God's strength released to deal with our weaknesses, and His omnipotence is released to deal with our impotence. The hallmark of a person who has prevailed in the spirit is that his vision of spiritual reality is never blurred by physical sight.

That person has the ability to walk through any physical barricade as though it does not exist. And indeed, where he is operating from—in the spirit—it does not exist. It's only a mirage, and that's what it is in reality. Consider the example of Elisha in Second Kings 6:8-23. When the army of Syria besieged the city that Elisha lived in, it took the elevated sight of Elisha to calm his troubled servant and gain the victory that had been ordained for him.

So David took his staff. Remember that he did not just pick any staff—he picked *his* staff. A staff is an instrument of authority conferred on the owner based on some work, associations, or achievement. This time it represents his authorization from God—the word that gave him the impetus to stand against Goliath. Now, understand that David knew the history of his people. He had a covenant and kept the covenant with his God. He kept the laws of God, honored his father, and took charge of responsibilities in the father's house.

In the present church formation, most times we are trying to pick up the staff of someone else to go against our Goliath. It just cannot work. The staff of your pastor or other people in places of authority over you can take you somewhere, but it will never make you arrive at destiny. One pertinent question we need to ask ourselves is: "Whose authority are we using?" If we do not submit fully to God, His Word, and spiritual oversight, there will be no conferment of authority to exercise authority effectively. The degree of your submission determines the degree of your authority.

David chose for himself five smooth stones from the brook. The brook represents a place of living water—the Word of God. We need to get the revealed word of God—*Rhema*—from the written Word—*logos*—represented by the five smooth stones. There is a general word of promise for every child of God, but until you have a word revealed to your spirit by the Holy Spirit you may still not be able to overcome. Until you have revelation knowledge of God's Word in a certain specific area of your life, the gates of hell will continue to prevail.

David was a man of covenant and the Word. He had taken time to build intimacy with God in the wilderness while taking care of the few sheep of his father. You should never despise the days of small beginning, as God judges faithfulness by looking at how you handle small things.

Long before I became a pastor, I used to leave my house every morning to water plants on the church grounds. I was consistent and faithful in that little thing, and God saw it and possibly said, "If she can take so much care for plants, I can trust her with people." Your promotion does not come from man.

> *For exaltation comes neither from the east nor from the west nor from the south. But God is the Judge: He puts down one, and exalts another* (Psalm 75:6-7).

If it required a person to call me into ministry, it would have taken forever. They just wouldn't see the potential on the inside. All they saw was my outward weakness, poverty, and flaws. But to get a clearer and fuller perspective of what is going on around a person, you need to go past all his apparent flaws, failures, and weaknesses. That is how Good looks. He does not look at the outward appearances, but He looks into the heart (see 1 Sam. 16:7).

David put the stones in a shepherd bag. His shepherd bag represents his experience, faithfulness, and commitment to his father. What are you doing in your father's house? If you cannot say categorically what you are doing, there will be nowhere to put the stones. In other words, no carrier, no container for that potent tool that God wants to use to deal with the enemy. It must be contained somewhere, because it is not for public view. It is private, and God is going to keep it hidden until you draw near to the enemy. The enemy must never have a view of what you are about to release. You must spring it suddenly at him. In warfare, three elements are needed for victory—speed, shock, and surprise—so you must never allow the enemy to come to you. David ran toward him. You must be thinking faster than the enemy can respond and always be the first on the attack.

The Sling

The believer's mouth is the sling that will eventually push the stone straight to where the enemy will be hardest hit. It is and always has been a war of words:

> *And He has made My mouth like a sharp sword; in the shadow of His hand He has hidden Me, and made Me a polished shaft; in His quiver He has hidden Me* (Isaiah 49:2).

Notice that it was the Philistine who first spoke. He made a terrible mistake of cursing David and his God. "When the enemy comes in like a flood, the Spirit of the Lord will lift up a standard against him" (Isa. 59:19). The Word is a standard that the spirit uses always. Goliath continued his war of words and intimidation by declaring that he was going to give David's flesh to the birds of the air.

> *And the Philistine said to David, "Come to me, and I will give your flesh to the birds of the air and the beasts of the field!"* (1 Samuel 17:44)

Notice that Goliath said "your flesh." He never said David's spirit. In the day we are living, all the enemy wants to use is fear of the death of the flesh. But the flesh has to die for the spirit to fully live.

A man of experience with God puts no confidence in the flesh and loves not his life until death. Until there is a generation who will rise up and say to the powers of darkness, "If I perish, I perish" like Esther (Esther 4:16), there can never be a true and lasting victory for the Church. For a long time, satan has used the fear of death to hold the Church down. Jesus declares in John 12, "He who loves his life will lose it, and he who hates his life in this world will keep it for eternal life" (John 12:25).

The Bible says the last enemy to be destroyed is death (see 1 Cor. 15:26). It is my belief and conviction that God will have a people on the earth who will be clothed with immortality while in the flesh and the fear of death will be completely erased from their subconscious minds. They will live in total and complete dominion over death, because they have taken time to be clothed with the life of God from their spirit, soul, and body. They will have total dominion.

David too did not keep his mouth shut, but he responded. You see, the enemy will first start the speaking through adverse situations, troubles, afflictions, and tribulations. But God forbid that you have no answer for him. No answer means that you are consenting to all he has said. Your response is the only thing that God can use to quench the fiery darts of the enemy. You must respond.

David's response sounded like this: "Hey! Goliath, you have misunderstood the nature of this battle before you. You are coming with the physical, which to me is a limitation in itself, but I am coming against you with the Limitless One who can use anything at His disposal or nothing at all to bring an end to your existence. His name is a Strong Tower, His name is the El Shaddai, His name is the Mighty God, and His name is the Man of War. Hey Goliath, He has your very breath in His hand. I will let you experience Him today, but you will not live to tell it on the earth. Hey Goliath, you can only fully comprehend the power of His wrath in hell; because not only does He have the power to remove you from the earth, He will also damn your soul in hell. Goliath, you have completely underestimated the power of the God of Israel. Goliath, this day I want the whole earth to know that the God of Israel is alive and well, for indeed it was never my battle but His."

You need to understand that everything happened within a few seconds. Often it is the speed of your response that determines the speed of your deliverance.

Sometimes we allow things to linger and the enemy speaks louder. That was the problem with Saul's army. Forty days, no response; forty days they were spellbound, forty days they hid in caves, forty days they looked each other on the face instead of looking the enemy in the face. Forty days they just had no response. What a state of hopelessness and helplessness. Was God in their camp? Could He have helped them? Was He happy with the taunts, reproach, and insults from Goliath? Was His hand short? Was He willing that they die in that valley of decision? Oh! That the salvation of Israel would come out of Zion, when the Lord will turn the captivity of His people around and give them fame in every land of shame.

But there was no man. He looked, and behold there was no man, and He wondered, "Why is there not a man?" So He sent a man to the camp. You see, what will qualify you to step into the camp and face Goliath is not the joining of Saul's army. It's the obedience to the Father and faithfulness in small things. David never went to seek Goliath; it came naturally in the course of his faithful obedience to his father. He was a true son. True sons are faithful in the house and willing to take care of those chores that seem beneath them. Remember that David was already anointed at this time to be king, but he did not deem it underneath his status to continue shepherding his father's flock.

Stepping Out

These days when one senses the anointing, the next place they head to is the pulpit or preaching ministry. It appears to be the place obvious to all, and therefore a place that seems to bring the most respect and glory. God is not interested in what we preach as much as who we are.

Sometimes I actually wish that God would have just made me an armor-bearer to someone else in the forefront, but I know that

God chooses to use anyone the way He deems fit. It has to do with God's purpose, and I'm just fulfilling what He has called me to do.

The pulpit ministry is in no way the most accomplished ministry. There are too many saints doing great exploits for God who will never be seen or even heard of by men, yet their footprints are firmly printed in the sands of time, and eternity will reveal the depths of their labor, and the reward and honor of the Master conferred on them will astound many.

These are secret disciples who are always there to provide the most critical need of the Master. Like Joseph of Arimathea—when the curtains fell and the apostles fled, he was bold to go to Pilate to demand the body of the Master. He provided a fitting burial place and fulfilled Scriptures. Scriptures have to be fulfilled, but who will cooperate with God to bring them to pass? God in all ages has always been looking for a man.

Why is there a dearth of men? Because there has to be processing; God will not just pick a man and pour His glory in him. No, glory cannot be contaminated by flesh. He needs "dead men," because they have ceased to talk. Their bodies no longer respond to anything physical; they are completely in the spirit. There is a dearth of men because many are not willing to be processed. It's extremely costly; it will cost everything they are. Their goals, their thoughts, their plans, their ambitions, their desires, their visions, their titles—every dimension of their flesh must die. It is far too expensive. But the suffering of the present is nothing compared to the glory that shall be revealed.

> *For our light affliction, which is but for a moment, is working for us a far more exceeding and eternal weight of glory, while we do not look at the things which are seen, but at the things which are not seen. For the things which are seen are temporary, but the things which are not seen are eternal* (2 Corinthians 4:17-18).

You see, the whole creation is now waiting to see the manifestation of a glorious people called the Sons of God. "Sons of God" simply means no effort from man or flesh. They have been processed by the spirit, sent to places in the spirit, incubated in the land of affliction, sent to the school of the wilderness, and have perfected the lot of total dependence on El Shaddai.

They have scars that show they have survived diverse battles and were not ashamed to be identified with the suffering of the Messiah. They died with Him and went through pains inexplicable, tears uncountable, and fears unlimited; they have been rejected and scorned by men. Pushed hard but not crushed, perplexed but not despairing, struck down not destroyed.

> We are hard-pressed on every side, yet not crushed; we are perplexed, but not in despair; persecuted, but not forsaken; struck down, but not destroyed—always carrying about in the body the dying of the Lord Jesus, that the life of Jesus also may be manifested in our body (2 Corinthians 4:8-10).

These are the vessels ready to contain the glory. For we have the treasure in earthen vessels. Until the gold of His nature has been beaten into the earthen vessel and the earthen vessel's identity is completely submerged in his golden image, only then can creation be liberated from the bondage of corruption.

Today there is so much corruption on planet Earth. Creation is groaning under the weight of evil, but until the standard of the Word and the spirit is lifted, only then can creation experience true liberty. In the heart of the Spirit, there is a cry for a man. There is an advertisement going on in the frequency of Heaven, blasting into the earth "Wanted! A man. Who will go for Me?" Until one recognizes the state of his impurity, he cannot demand for the coal from the altar (see Isa. 6:6-7). A self-sufficient man in his righteousness is the most deluded man. Our sufficiency must be of Him if our relevance and purpose must be achieved.

David responded and the Bible records he had no sword in his hands. Whenever you go out in faith to deal with the enemy—either to get back a stolen territory, your health, or other things—you must understand that the very tool he has tried to use for your destruction is the very tool you will use to decapitate him. When the stone hit Goliath on the one spot that was never covered, he fell down but did not die.

Things to note:

1. God knows the loophole the enemy has created or left for his destruction. A great number of times, after we have exploited the loophole and hit the enemy by God's wisdom, he only falls down, but is not dead.

2. To finish the work and make sure there will be no breath for him again, you need to take that same weapon that was in his hand and finish the work. Whatever weapon he had is what God intends for you to use to put an eternal end to his onslaught.

So David ran and stood over the Philistine (Goliath), took his sword, drew it out of its sheath, killed him, and cut off his head with it. This is the posture of a true victorious person.

In my opinion, Goliath lost his mind when he went against David. How could his sword be still in its sheath? Why couldn't he draw it out? Guess what happened—he was paralyzed from brain to hand. When God goes before you into battle, He makes the enemies begin to act illogically. They become confused. Whenever God really wants to bless you in life with abundance of gold, silver, and all, He will allow a multitude to come against you overdressed for the battle so that you will go like Jehoshaphat and strip their corpses of all the jewelries.

> *When Jehoshaphat and his people came to take away their spoil, they found among them an abundance of valuables on the dead bodies, and precious jewelry, which they stripped off for themselves, more than they could carry away; and*

they were three days gathering the spoil because there was so much (2 Chronicles 20:25).

When the Philistines saw that their champion was dead, they fled. To tell you the truth, as long as a strong man is armed and keeps his house his goods are secure, but it will take a stronger man to disarm him and spoil his goods. At the flight of the Philistines, the army of Israel that was paralyzed for forty days got their strength renewed. It will take a catalyst like David to bring the Church out of the state of stupor, paralysis, and outright impotence. It took David to get them pursuing after the Philistines. The Church needs leaders who will be ready to pay the price and bring victory to the armies of God on the earth.

God's Army

The Church is God's army, but the Church today is an army in civilian attire and lacks the disciplines that ensure victory. Many of the so-called commanders are inexperienced babes. In the spiritual, all the enemy sees are babes, dressed in their diapers, carrying guns so potent, yet unskilled in the very act of warfare and above all turning the guns on one another. When there are schisms, divisions, envies, and all kinds of evil in the Church, the enemy just watches as they devour each other. What the Church should really be binding today is not the devil but the Church itself. The Church should bind itself to the will of God, to the purpose of God, and to the ways of God, and we will have fewer demons to bind.

David took the head of the Philistine and brought it to Jerusalem, but he put his armor in his tent. David knew the head of the Philistine was not his personal victory, so he took it to where it belonged. Our victory is not just our personal victory but that of the Church of Jesus Christ.

Our perspective of purpose must be redefined if we will ever fully fulfill it. Purpose is beyond me and you. It has to do with

God, creation, and people. David knew beyond an iota of a doubt that he had nothing to do with that victory. God brought victory to His people through a man. That has been it from the beginning. God has always raised a man for a people. David put Goliath's armor in his tent. That was to serve as a reminder to him that the man who wore this armor was a dead man and never to attempt to put on armor tailored by the world and the flesh.

The weapons of our warfare and even the armor (protective covering) are not carnal (natural) but are mighty through God to the pulling down of satanic strongholds (see 2 Cor. 10:4). A stronghold is a thought, an imagination or idea that has gripped one's mind and thereby controls one's attitudes and actions. Satan uses it as a potent tool to take people captive and hold them by it. As long as satanic strongholds abound in one's imagination, the entire life of such a person is under the control and manipulation of the enemy; and until it is knocked down by the truth in God's Word, such a person has little or no chance for freedom and liberty in those areas.

The Philistine giant had brought a griping fear on the camp of Israel, and it became a stronghold that told them, "None of you can face this giant." So a man had to come with a new mindset and faith in God.

> *When Saul saw David going out against the Philistine, he said to Abner, the commander of the army, "Abner, whose son is this youth?" And Abner said, "As your soul lives, O king, I do not know"* (1 Samuel 17:55).

In this day, what will show you off is your ability to stay under a true and tested fatherhood and be trained. It takes the Spirit of the Father conferred on an obedient son for the world to acknowledge that God lives. Whose son are you? Let me say that we all say God is our Father, but the truth is He is not a Father to all. He asked Israel, "If I be a Father, then where is My honor?"

> *A son honors his father, and a servant his master. If then I am the Father, where is My honor? And if I am a Master, where is My reverence? Says the Lord of hosts to you priests who despise My name. Yet you say, "In what way have we despised Your name?"* (Malachi 1:6)

Until we live our lives with the manifestations of the true nature and character of God, we lie. Until our lives have His DNA (Divine Nature Attributes), we are none of His. Until we have His Spirit, we belong to another.

Perhaps I need to also say here that there is an issue of spiritual fatherhood in the Church that has to be properly addressed. Someone is not your spiritual father because you got born again in their church, just as it's not possible for one to claim parenthood because a child was born in his home. For one to be a father he must have ministered to your spirit and you must have received his spirit—lifestyle and attitudes. You cannot claim someone is your father if you do not look like them. Until you have received the disciplines and corrections of spiritual oversight, do not claim them as fathers.

There are as few fathers in the Body of Christ today as they are few true sons. God said that unless He corrects and discipline us, we are bastards. "But if you are without chastening, of which all have become partakers, then you are illegitimate and not sons" (Heb. 12:8).

One cannot underscore the importance of true sonship in the Body of Christ today. The whole creation is waiting for the manifestation of sons, not children. An heir cannot inherit as long as he is a child. The promised land is not for children but sons. When Saul asked whose son David was, Abner the commander could not tell. See, it is not for others to tell whose son you are. You are the only one who can declare unambiguously by your deeds whose son you are. So David prevailed against the giant of the Philistines and brought glory to the God of Heaven, even the God of Israel. What an awesome feat of faith.

POINTS TO PONDER

1. God is looking for a man who can step out and challenge His enemies.

2. Saul's type of leadership has no answer for the challenges facing the Church today. Those who cannot discover God for themselves cannot teach the people how to.

3. You cannot win a spiritual battle with a physical weapon, and you must never compromise with the enemy. Compromise kills destiny.

4. Prayer must return to the Church and the Church must learn to open her mouth wide, because ours is a war of words.

Chapter 5

David's Men: Ordinary Men Called to a New Destiny

David's Men: Ordinary Men Called to a New Destiny

The present Church must fully come to terms with the fact that nothing much will be achieved by individual grace and anointing. The only way we can truly defeat the god of this world and turn the kingdoms over to Christ is through our corporate strength.

David killed the giant of the Philistine, but there were still other battles and giants to contend with. Just because you've overcome in one war doesn't mean the battles are over. You can ask the Americans in Iraq. The war was declared officially over, but every day they had to fight insurgencies here and there. So also is the nature of our spiritual warfare. Satan is an outlaw, and he has been declared a loser but never gives up. So David understood that God had raised him up to champion the cause of his people and got submitted to Saul. Let me say here that even though David had been anointed as king, Saul was still the official king of Israel, and any acts of rebellion on the part of David would have been a limitation to his ascension to his throne or more still his own demise on the throne.

When God says anything about you, wait for the time. When He has anointed you for any work, wait for the time. If you must fight to ascend to where God has promised you, then be careful to let Him do the fighting through you. Not by your power, might, or skill.

Trust, dependence on God, and the greatest virtue of all—*patience*—cannot be over-emphasized. So David stayed under Saul until Saul's jealously and rage got to an alarming and unacceptable life-threatening dimension, then David left Saul's house. Even then he did not stir up insurgency against Saul, neither did he instigate others. He just ran away.

Let God Fight the Battle

The man who must ascend to the position God has promised should never fight to remove anyone from their own positions. It is with the same measure you give that it shall be measured back to you. Had David done that, Absalom his son would have succeeded in his rebellion against David. Do you understand how these things work? You who say "an eye for an eye," there is a higher commandment than that of limited judgment. Take not vengeance; it belongs to God, and He will repay.

In my walk with God, I have come to the understanding that the battles we fight are not necessarily ours but the Lord's, and the actual enemy is the devil. The devil has a way of confronting human vessels, so we cannot take our eyes off him—the real enemy. When you decide not to deal with the human channels in vengeance, God deals with the real enemy on your behalf and brings glory to Himself.

It is not the will of God that any man should perish. Christ died for all. Human vessels are desperately in need of deliverance. David found himself running to the wilderness and living in a cave after escaping from the land of the Philistines.

The man God will ultimately use for His glory has to be processed in the place of trials and afflictions. Trials are a necessary part of processing. Gold cannot assume its finest quality until it goes through the furnace. This is not a place you want to go, but can the clay say to the potter, "Why am I like this?" You have to understand that the fire is not for your destruction but for construction.

David had received an anointing, and the anointing has a way of attracting. But who were those attracted to David? Everyone who was in distress, everyone who was in debt, and everyone who was discontented, including his father's house and his brethren.

> *David therefore departed from there and escaped to the cave of Adullam. And when his brothers and all his father's house heard it, they went down there to him. And everyone who was in distress, everyone who was in debt, and everyone who was discontented gathered to him. So he became captain over them. And there were about four hundred men with him* (1 Samuel 22:1-2).

This is a lesson to all pastors. Sometimes we want the rich and mighty to come to us so we can be captain over them. The rich and mighty will never allow you to be a true captain over them. You cannot rule over people who feel they have more than you.

> *For you see your calling, brethren, that not many wise according to the flesh, not many mighty, not many noble, are called* (1 Corinthians 1:26).

When God brings the rejected and "scum," as it were, whose total offerings cannot pay your fare back to your house, what do you do with them? The hallmark of a truly anointed captain is that he will begin to impact and transform the lives of his followers. Anointing without impartation is no good, and to impact lives, your life must first be impacted; you cannot give what you do not have.

David had to stay under the tutelage of God to receive daily provisions and instruction for his followers. They were needy people, but God had a plan. To possess the land it will have to take a corporate effort, and this is one lesson the Church of the twenty-first century has to quickly learn. The world has perfected the act of corporate image and achievement, but the Church has not. No one man can finish the work by himself. No one pastor can take the Church to her ultimate position. The corporate Church needs the five-fold ministries of the apostles, prophets, evangelists, pastors, and teachers to rise up.

> *Till we all come to the unity of the faith and of the knowledge of the Son of God, to a perfect man, to the measure of the stature of the fullness of Christ* (Ephesians 4:13).

So all these men were gathered to David and were submitted to him as a leader over them. Let me say that true leadership is not something forced on people. People will be willing to submit if they see these qualities in their leader—selflessness, compassion, vision, insight, foresight, and, above all, love. Excellent leaders add value to their people and help them become better than they would ever be on their own.

David loved the people. He not only cared for them but was understanding and compassionate to their cause. This was what enabled him to act in wisdom toward all his men. Of course David's men had their own problems, just like the twelve apostles of Jesus had, but love kept them together. When the followership sees love in their leadership, then they will do anything for that leadership. David's men were loyal and faithful to him, and that enabled them to begin their journey into the fulfillment of purpose.

People of Purpose

Every purpose of God starts with a man but ends with a people. The man Moses was called, but he ended with a company of Israelites. Abraham was called, but he ended with a company of nations of people. The promises of God will always come to one person but ultimately transcend him. God is looking for a man, but His covenant is with a people. In other words, the man God seeks must possess the ability to multiply himself. When man was created, he was instructed by God to multiply and replenish the earth. Every leader must possess the capacity to multiply himself in his followership. Success without a successor is no success after all. Perhaps all leaders need to ask themselves from time to time what they are transferring to their followership. Followership that has not also inculcated the discipline and lifestyle of the leader cannot endure. Any wind of change will blow them anywhere and everywhere. Moreover, until leadership plants disciplines into followership, neither can expect to reach their full potential. It takes one man to receive a promise but a company to inherit the fullness of the promise.

So David knew if he was to ascend the throne he needed the company of people who voluntarily came to him. But these were weak, poor, discontented, indebted, and distressed people. You wonder how this group can ever make it. You see, that is the difference between a man anointed and called by God and one appointed by men. It took an anointing to transform ignorant men like Peter and John and give then the boldness to resist the Pharisees and the Sadducees of their days. It took the anointing on Jesus to bring them to that. It took the anointing on David to transform his men and himself. Remember that the anointing flows from the head, and what the head does not possess the body cannot receive.

David had an obligation under God to bring transformation to the lives of his followers of about four hundred men. One would assume that when Samuel anointed David as king over Israel, the whole nation full of riches and wealth would be endowed on him, but here we see the anointing represented the exact opposite.

David was now a captain of four hundred—not four million or even four hundred thousand—but a careful selection of "rejects." Oh, the God we serve. He takes pleasure in using the useless things to confound the "useful," the foolish to confound the wise, and the weak to confound the strong. No flesh can glory in His sight. He proves to His people that though your beginnings are small, your end shall be great. He proves He is a God of fidelity and truth to give us an understanding that everything must gradually grow to fulfill its end.

The seed grows from the blade to the ear, and then the full corn develops in the ear. Anything that has no gradual growth has no lasting life. The longer it takes some things to grow, the longer it will also take to die. An example is a palm tree. It takes years to grow and mature, but it can outlast a generation of people. *Selah* (think about this).

Over the years of being a pastor, I have discovered that God brings people who will submit to my leadership as a pastor, and no matter how crooked or twisted their lives have been they always turn things around for the best. I do not go out to seek people who have it all worked out, because such have no glory to offer to God but their achievements and connections. But when a man has lost all his connections, all he had, and is even at the point of losing his mind, when God brings a complete turnaround he will give all glory to God.

So David was captain over a people who in the natural had nothing to offer him but in the spiritual possessed tremendous wealth and power. He had a choice—leave them and not bother with them and seek his welfare from the kings of Moab and the Philistines, or gather them around him and impact their lives. To be able to impact the lives of your followership, they must actively participate with you in your daily routines.

David had experiences with God as a shepherd boy, and he needed to "download" the same from his spirit to his followers. These experiences gave him victory with the bear, the lion, and ultimately with Goliath. Let me say that until a leader can impact a few he should never expect much from God. Sometimes pastors pray for their fold to increase, but what have they done with the ones they have?

It is not really about the size of your flock, but how well they look. A few healthy sheep are far more valuable than a herd of sick, blind, and lame animals. I believe the Church is full of the sick, the lame, and the blind sheep, and it's the duty of the pastors to see that they are healed, delivered, and freed to live healthy lives spiritually, physically, mentally, and materially. Now there is a two-fold problem within the Church:

1. The sheep come to church without understanding how precarious their state is. I dare to say wolves also come, but dressed like sheep.
2. Some pastors really do not care about the sheep's well-being, but only about fleecing the sheep.

When you have a pastor who cares, then the sheep have to submit totally to the instruction, leadership, and guidance of such a pastor or they will never attain their full status and well-being. The pastor has a responsibility to tell the whole truth to the people and to discipline where necessary. As long as the sheep do what they want, eat what they what, drink what they want, sleep with what they want (including dogs, mad men, and women), come to church when they want, and give offerings when they want and how they want, they will remain, sick, lame, and blind for all time and eternity.

A Disciplined Flock

Discipline is a key word that must return to the vocabulary of the Church. The pastor has a duty to protect the flock from wolves. Wolves are there to kill, maim, and devour the sheep. Anyone who comes to church and stays steeped in sin with a hard heart toward repentance is a wolf and must be prayerfully sent out. Over the years, wolves have been disconnected from the church where God has set me as an overseer, but not by my power. Sometimes, after a period of fasting and prayer, some people will naturally leave church. If you ask them why, they simply cannot logically defend their stand. God told them to leave so that it will be apparent to all that they were never a part. If they were a part, they would remain (see 2 Pet. 2). When a pastor has people who refuse to obey God's and man's instructions, refuse to live holy lives, and refuse to pray and just live in rebellion to all sound doctrine, you should know you are dealing with witches or wolves.

Witches are in churches. The Bible says rebellion is as the sin of witchcraft. The only way to rid the Body of Christ of witchcraft is to pray for the people to repent or be sent out by the fire of God, period! "Suffer not a witch to live" is still the standard. The wages of sin have never changed. If nothing is done about the rebellious, they will continue to leech on others and steal life out of the genuine sheep, thereby wearing them out or even killing them spiritually. We need strong sheep so they can reproduce after their kind.

David fed his men spiritually and physically. When he sent to Nabal, it wasn't for his needs—it was for his men. Any pastor who does not take care of the needs of his flock until they become strong enough to take care of themselves should not expect to take from them when they are strong. In fact, they will never arrive at their maximum potential. The pastor must care enough to get from the rich and affluent through his personal faith in order to help the congregation grow.

There's only so much you can fleece from a sheep. If there's no wool, there's really no wool. Feed the sheep, take care of them, grow them well, and surely your harvest will come. There were times I had to surrender tithes and offerings to meet the needs of church members, and I still do because we all are at different stages of spiritual development and maturity. And God has always been faithful to meet my needs and the needs of the church. One of the things that never ceased to amaze me is the fact that I have not paid any rent for any property we have ever used for fellowship for sixteen years, and that is favor.

When you take care of the flock, God will take care of you. It is that simple. You take care of and grow the flock; God takes care of and grows you up. And the more the capacity of your spirit man enlarges, the more wealth, power, and glory you access. Any other way is called a shortcut, and in the things of the spirit the shortcut is always the longest way, ultimately. What you have not confronted must come back to confront you.

David's men were with him from the wilderness throughout his journeys in the land of the Philistines. They shared in his pains, affliction, and sorrows. If men stay with you and remain loyal in your times of nothingness, then they also will be partakers of your glory. "To the extent that you partake of Christ's sufferings, that when His glory is revealed, you may also be glad with exceeding joy" (1 Pet. 4:13). Some want the glory without the suffering. You cannot be a true partaker of the glory without first partaking of the sufferings.

It is time the Body of Christ is told that to get the crown without the Cross is a satanic message and not the Gospel of the Kingdom. Let the people of God depart from this culture of deception. When satan offered Jesus the glory, trying to bypass the Cross and the sufferings, Jesus rejected it. There was and there is still is a pattern. Jesus learned obedience through suffering. "Though He was a Son, yet He learned obedience by the things which He suffered" (Heb 5:8). God has designed that perfection will be achieved through sufferings. So why is the Church not preaching the Passion?

I believe in total prosperity, but not without the Passion—you must know Him in the fellowship of His sufferings to be partakers of His resurrection power. I usually look past the glamour and the glory in God's people to the scars underneath. Every servant anointed by God has a story to tell, that's why it is not wise to want to be like another. You may not be well-equipped or capable of handling their pains. Just be you. Grace to be all you can be is available to you, and it's tailored to fit your circumstances.

David and his men continued in the wilderness under very stringent situations, but God was with them. It is not where you are in life that really counts but who is with you. If God is for you, no one can be against you. He says, "I can make the wilderness to become a pool of water and your dry land springs of living water."

Joseph was in prison but God was with him, so even though he was in prison, prison never got inside of him. Greater is He who is in you than he who is outside.

I need to say that every man of God must have a wilderness experience. Your actions, attitude, response, and reaction will determine how long you stay there or whether you will die there. Amazingly, only two men out of over 600,000 who left Egypt in that older generation made it past the wilderness; the rest died there. The Bible records that it was eleven days' journey from Egypt to the threshold of the Promised Land, but it took Israel forty years. Why?

The wilderness represents a place of dealing with God that is designed to rid you of Egyptian and slave mentalities, to give you a new mindset of who God is and how truly awesome and great He is. It's a place where God deals with human dependence on self and things, and God experientially becomes the *El Shaddai* and *Jehovah Jireh* to us. It is a place for supernatural supply.

God permitted Israel to go to Egypt for preservation and sustenance, but they had a culture and most especially a covenant with God that distinguished them from the Egyptians. Though you are in the world, you are not part of the world. The Bible states that to love the world and conform to it is to be an enemy of God. So in the wilderness, God's intention is to get rid of any residual enmity between Him and us by teaching us true dependence on Him. Israel missed God because they murmured, complained, and lusted exceedingly in the wilderness.

> *And all the children of Israel complained against Moses and Aaron, and the whole congregation said to them, "If only we had died in the land of Egypt! Or if only we had died in this wilderness!"* (Numbers 14:2)

Be careful that you do not murmur and complain about the dealings of God; just learn the lessons and move on. His intentions are good and wholesome for you. All murmurers and complainers died in the wilderness. Jesus went into the wilderness led by the Spirit but returned in the power of the Spirit.

Then Jesus, being filled with the Holy Spirit, returned from the Jordan and was led by the Spirit into the wilderness (Luke 4:1).

The wilderness can either be a place of recuperation or death; it's all a matter of your attitude. Jesus was tempted with thirst and hunger, but He did not lust or allow satan to use His hunger to instigate Him against God. He knew that man does not live by bread alone. Most times when God is trying to teach us total dependence on Him and increase our faith, we get confused about His dealings and begin to complain and murmur. This should not be.

Understand that all He is trying to do is to take you to a place where you will be free from all natural entanglement, where nothing can be used by the enemy as bait to draw you from purpose.

Learning Dependence

I remember the early days of my Christianity when the Lord was teaching me faith and dependence on Him. Any time I had no money in my hand, I would pray and pray and pray until one day the Lord said to me, "I did not create money; it is a means of exchange for goods or services and I can give you both without money." It sounded a little crazy to me because of my level of faith at that time, but let God be true and every man be a liar. The next time I had to go somewhere and I had no money for my fares, the Lord took me to the Scripture in Psalm 50:10: "Every beast of the forest is Mine, and the cattle on a thousand hills." In other words, I could take any car to wherever I wanted.

I stepped out of my house and waved down an approaching car. What happened amazed me. It would be normal for a driver of the car to open the car door for me. But instead, the owner of the car came out from the back seat and opened the door for me and took me to where I was going, and from that day the fear of "no money no going places" was broken.

I have had to take an offering at the airport to get my ticket. You might say, "Such boldness!" But you were created to dominate your circumstances and not allow them to determine your direction in life. Your wilderness experience is to teach you that you can have and do all things through Christ. The Bible records that the Israelites' clothes and shoes did not get old. In other words, their shoes were growing with their feet—amazing. There were no supermarkets, but they were eating well. God gave them angels' food.

The problem was they wanted to have their own kind of food the Egyptian way—lettuce, cucumbers, onions, garlic—these are all symbolic. It simply means that when God is taking you on a journey to greatness, your appetites and taste buds have to change. The "diet" of Egypt can never take you to your promised land. The company you used to keep cannot take you into purpose with God.

When a woman gets pregnant and is about to bring a new life into the earth, her appetites must of necessity change; her walk will change, her posture changes, indeed even her dressing must change because her normal clothes will not fit her present size and posture. So also, when we start a journey with God, we get pregnant with the seed of His Son, and if we do not adhere to our Doctor's instructions, we will abort. A lot of Christians have long aborted the purposes of God for their lives. Some still manage to carry to full term but have missed the mark, thereby giving birth to "Ichabods"—no glory.[1]

Any so-called work we are doing for God that cannot give glory to God but seeks to exalt men and their egos will not pass the test of God. Sin is a reproach. Sin is simply missing the mark. Anything that did not make the mark is *sin*, no matter how good it appears before men. That's why Jesus said, "In that day many shall say 'I cast out demons in Your name, I healed in Your name' but I will say to them 'depart from Me, ye workers of iniquity (sin)'" (see Matt. 7:22-23).

What was sinful about casting out devils and curing people? The truth was that their works did not bring glory to God. They puffed up their ministries and made them popular with men, but they were not according to the plan and purpose of God.

God said to Moses, "Make sure you build according to the pattern shown to you on the mount." So there is a pattern, and any deviation from it is called sin (see Exod. 25:40).

In the Wilderness

Any and every person who God uses must necessarily have a wilderness experience. Without it, you cannot know God nor comprehend His ways. For His ways are not our ways or His thoughts our thoughts. David and his men were in the wilderness, but God was with them. It is the anointing that preserves you wherever you are. While David and his men were in the wilderness, God was busy training them in the art of warfare. He gathered these fearful men to attack the Philistines and save the city of Keilah.

They could not remain in the city, because the inhabitants would have delivered David to Saul. It was not so much the plan of the enemy as the purpose of God that kept them on the run. God will always use the enemy's schemes to take us where He wants us.

> *Then they told David, saying, "Look, the Philistines are fighting against Keilah, and they are robbing the threshing floors." Therefore David inquired of the Lord, saying, "Shall I go and attack these Philistines?" And the Lord said to David, "Go and attack the Philistines, and save Keilah." But David's men said to him, "Look, we are afraid here in Judah. How much more then if we go to Keilah against the armies of the Philistines?"* (1 Samuel 23:1-3)

So he moved on, but they were still in the wilderness. How long you remain in the wilderness is largely determined by:

1. The purpose of God
2. Your attitude

David was running from one wilderness to another because Saul was out to kill him. Eventually, he allied with the Philistines.

> *And David said in his heart, "Now I shall perish someday by the hand of Saul. There is nothing better for me than that I should speedily escape to the land of the Philistines; and Saul will despair of me, to seek me anymore in any part of Israel. So I shall escape out of his hand." Then David arose and went over with the six hundred men who were with him to Achish the son of Maoch, king of Gath. So David dwelt with Achish at Gath, he and his men, each man with his household, and David with his two wives, Ahinoam the Jezreelitess, and Abigail the Carmelitess, Nabal's widow. And it was told Saul that David had fled to Gath; so he sought him no more. Then David said to Achish, "If I have now found favor in your eyes, let them give me a place in some town in the country, that I may dwell there. For why should your servant dwell in the royal city with you?" So Achish gave him Ziklag that day. Therefore Ziklag has belonged to the kings of Judah to this day. Now the time that David dwelt in the country of the Philistines was one full year and four months (1 Samuel 27:1-7).*

Sixteen months he stayed there, and by now four hundred men have become six hundred. Let me say that any pastor who wants to see a crowd of thousands when he has not taken time to learn spiritual warfare, discipline, and diligence is only gathering the wind. You may get the thousands, but for how long can you rule?

By aligning with the Philistines, he got a city called Ziklag. Sometimes, when we do things against the purpose and the nature of God because of fear, we seem to get results, but how long can that last? What God has not done cannot endure. The heat of the fire will one day come, and the city God did not give you or build will be razed. That's exactly what happened to Ziklag.

Amalek is a type of the flesh. David should not have aligned with God's enemies in the first place. So the flesh came back to take whatever "good" the enemy gave. This is a vital lesson for any man God chooses and has anointed to lead His people. It was the fear of dying at the hand of Saul that drove him to align with the enemy.

Compromise with the enemy can achieve a quick result but certainly not an enduring or lasting one. When Ziklag was burned, God made sure that no lives were lost. The works of the flesh will be burned, but the people will escape.

> *Each one's work will become clear; for the Day will declare it, because it will be revealed by fire; and the fire will test each one's work, of what sort it is. If anyone's work which he has built on it endures, he will receive a reward. If anyone's work is burned, he will suffer loss; but he himself will be saved, yet so as through fire* (1 Corinthians 3:13-15).

This was one of the most distressful times in the life of David as his own people were prepared to stone him. Thanks to God who will not allow our errors to consume us but will always deliver us in spite of them. God said to him, "Pursue for you shall surely overtake them and without fail, recover all" (1 Sam. 30:8). Of the six hundred men, only four hundred could go with him to cross the brook Besor. The rest stayed behind.

Stick to His Plan

As a pastor for more than fifteen years, I have come to understand that not everyone in your congregation will be able to produce maximally in a time of need; nevertheless, the rest are still vital in keeping their eyes on the baggage. Not everyone can pray as you can or give as you can, but everyone can do something and everyone is important.

Sometimes there is a tendency to just ignore those whom you think are not producing as much or moving at your pace, but everyone is key in the advancement to Zion. They may not all advance at the same speed and time, but if they stay long enough and you care enough for them, they will all be partakers of the glory. I heard about a man who or seventeen years was not producing any results in his church—no good to the congregation and no good to the pastor. Then suddenly he approached his pastor and asked if a car could be given to him to bring people to church. His pastor was skeptical but decided to try him out. This man began to fill that car with the people he personally ministered to and brought them to church every Sunday. As the crowd was growing, he would make two or three trips to church every Sunday. Eventually he was given a van, then a bus. Today, he is the pastor of his former pastor's church. Some people are slow starters, but no pastor should underestimate the hand of God upon any person who is always there, even if they seem to be doing nothing.

David understood this, so when the wicked and worthless men who went with him decided the ones who stayed behind should not partake in the spoils, David rebuked them. David was a man with a generous spirit. He even extended the spoils to his friends and the elders of Judah.

> *Then all the wicked and worthless men of those who went with David answered and said, "Because they did not go with us, we will not give them any of the spoil that we have recovered, except for every man's wife and children, that they may lead them away and depart"* (1 Samuel 30:22).

The hallmark of a true man of God is that he has a free and generous spirit. A covetous man is only deceiving himself if he calls himself man of God. He is indeed a "man of satan." Satan is the one who wants to keep men in bondage, poverty, and lack; God gives freely all good things (see James 1:17 and Rom. 8:32).

While David was busy allowing God's dealings in his life, God was also making sure that the throne was getting close to being vacant. Sometimes, instead of minding our business with God, we begin to mind God's own for Him.

Then Samuel took the horn of oil and anointed him in the midst of his brothers; and the Spirit of the Lord came upon David from that day forward. So Samuel arose and went to Ramah (1 Samuel 16:13).

The idea of the throne was never David's; it was God's. If you mind the dealings, God will cause the throne to be vacant so you can assume your rulership as He has spoken. His word can never return to Him void. It must accomplish His pleasure.

For as the rain comes down, and the snow from heaven, and do not return there, but water the earth, and make it bring forth and bud, that it may give seed to the sower and bread to the eater, so shall My word be that goes forth from My mouth; it shall not return to Me void, but it shall accomplish what I please, and it shall prosper in the thing for which I sent it (Isaiah 55:10-11).

Saul and his sons came to a tragic end. One of the most pathetic stories I know in the Bible is the end of Jonathan, Saul's son. He knew about the anointing in the life of David, he prophesied that David would be king and he, Jonathan, would be next to him, but he lacked the disciplines to make the transition. He went to meet David in the wilderness, but the comfort of Saul's palace kept beckoning to him. He had to return to that comfort.

What a pity when we can see the great future ahead of us but become too lethargic and complacent to grasp the opportunities given to us by God. Opportunities always come dressed in work clothes, but if you can do the work you can get the crown. If you can pick the cross, take the walk, and bear the shame, reproach, insults, and misunderstandings of men, then you will see your prophecies fulfilled.

Looking unto Jesus, the author and finisher of our faith, who for the joy that was set before Him endured the cross, despising the shame, and has sat down at the right hand of the throne of God (Hebrews 12:2).

Oh! What a double tragedy it was for Jonathan. Now, I want you to pause here. Take a look at your life. What has been prophesied about you? What have you prophesied about yourself? Let me say that the Kingdom of God is not in words but in the demonstration of His power. No matter what has been prophesied, it will take you working it out with God to arrive at your destiny. You will not simply arrive without a process. However, if you do put in the work, you will reap the bountiful rewards.

Discipline must return to the Church. In the times of old, great men were men of character and discipline, but now many in the Church want to arrive in greatness without both. God cannot be mocked. The Bible says that what a man sows, that he reaps (see Gal. 6:7).

You get results proportional to your input and labor, unless you are a cheater. A student who wants to make straight As must be willing to pay the price to sit down, read, study, and do his tutorials.

The tradition of the Church must be broken if God is to rule in the midst of His people and scatter their enemies. The issue of being a pastor because you are next in line or in favor with the general overseer is a Philistine culture. Remember, it is the anointing that promotes and preserves. Israel wanted a king to be like the other nations. It was not God who said that they needed a king.

Our needs are different from our wants. When God sees a need, He supplies; when He sees your want, He cautions. Had they listened to Samuel, then they would have been spared the evil and traumatic rule of King Saul.

When Saul died, only the tribe of Judah anointed David king over them, but God said he would be king over Israel. It is vital to note that God will progressively take you closer to your destiny if you let Him. Be content with your status for now. It is all a matter of time. Godliness with contentment is great gain. Do not try to do the work of God for Him; wait for His plans to develop.

Ishbosheth was king, but God was still behind the scenes, working a way for David. Suddenly, a spirit of suspicion came into Ishbosheth, and he accused his commander of meddling with his concubine. The lesson here is that when God is about to do something concerning His promise for your life, the best allies can become enemies. So Abner, in anger, joined forces with David, but Joab, one of the mighty men of David, killed Abner. Isbosheth was murdered; confusion abounded.

> Now it was so, while there was war between the house of Saul and the house of David, that Abner was strengthening his hold on the house of Saul. And Saul had a concubine, whose name was Rizpah, the daughter of Aiah. So Ishbosheth said to Abner, "Why have you gone in to my father's concubine?" Then Abner became very angry at the words of Ishbosheth, and said, "Am I a dog's head that belongs to Judah? Today I show loyalty to the house of Saul your father, to his brothers, and to his friends, and have not delivered you into the hand of David; and you charge me today with a fault concerning this woman? May God do so to Abner, and more also, if I do not do for David as the Lord has sworn to him—to transfer the kingdom from the house of Saul, and set up the throne of David over Israel and over Judah, from Dan to Beersheba." And he could not answer Abner another word, because he feared him. Then Abner sent messengers on his behalf to David, saying, "Whose is the land?" saying also, "Make your covenant with me, and indeed my hand shall be with you to bring all Israel to you" (2 Samuel 3:6-12).

What in the natural looked like confusion was actually a divine ordering by God. Perhaps we need to look at moments like Ezekiel in the valley of dry bones. There's a lot of noise rattling just after you have prophesied. No need to be alarmed—the flesh is coming onto the bones.

So all the seeming confusion brought David to become king over Israel at last. One battle over, there were many more to be won. There is still more to come. Go along with Him. He is faithful.

> *Now there was a long war between the house of Saul and the house of David. But David grew stronger and stronger, and the house of Saul grew weaker and weaker* (2 Samuel 3:1).

There was a long war between the house of Saul and the house of David. But David ultimately became king over all Israel. Many times it looks as though the promises God has given or the anointing He has poured out was all in vain. Our natural circumstances go in the opposite direction of our expectations of the word of promise. In my experience, the promise must undergo the process. When the promises undergo the process of death and decay, then they are resurrected with a new life. It becomes impossible for anything to kill them. Through this avenue, God is positioned to bring the promised provision. If your vision has not undergone a process of death and been resurrected by God, anything can kill it at any time. But that which God has bought back from death, no man and no devil can kill.

The Process

Joseph had a similar situation. He was told by God in a series of dreams that he would rule over his brothers. The moment the vision was received, his circumstances began to take a turn for the "worse," but God was in it. The Bible records that God sent him to Egypt ahead of his brothers and family to preserve them from death.

> *But now, do not therefore be grieved or angry with yourselves because you sold me here; for God sent me before you to preserve life. For these two years the famine has been in*

> *the land, and there are still five years in which there will be neither plowing nor harvesting. And God sent me before you to preserve a posterity for you in the earth, and to save your lives by a great deliverance* (Genesis 45:5-7).

Now, here is the wisdom of God displayed, and it acted in two ways.

1. To fulfill His word in the fullness of time.
2. To strip the arrogant boy of his pride and build the character of God in him.

Let me also say that until we undergo the process that births character and humility in us, the promise may be delayed. God does not have any intention of bringing you to a place of promise to turn and fight or resist you. For He resists the proud but gives grace to the humble (see James 4:6).

When the character of God, which includes the highest form of humility, is not birthed in you, you will ultimately abuse and misuse the power given to you to help humanity. Joseph was raised up for a nation; it was not for his sake. Sometimes we think that God is blessing us just for us. Nonsense, it is the selfish nature of man that makes a man to misappropriate the blessings and prosperity that God gives. It is from God to all men, especially your brethren. Notice that all Egypt was kept alive because of the wisdom of Joseph, but it was primarily to keep the descendants of Abraham so that God could fulfill his promise to Abraham. In other words, when you allow God to work out His will and plans in you, even the whole world will partake in your blessings.

> *Let Pharaoh do this, and let him appoint officers over the land, to collect one-fifth of the produce of the land of Egypt in the seven plentiful years. And let them gather all the food of those good years that are coming, and store up grain under the authority of Pharaoh, and let them keep food in the cities. Then that food shall be as a reserve for the land for the seven years of famine which shall be in the land of*

Egypt that the land may not perish during the famine (Genesis 41:34-36).

Oh, the faithfulness of God.

The patriarch Abraham also had to undergo a process of learning to build character and allowing his dream to die. He started off as Abram, the exalted father, but ended up Abraham, the father of many nations. As long as you are the exalted father, you cannot be the father of many nations, because you have already usurped the position of God. And anything that takes the position of God is an idol, and idols are dumb and unproductive. So Abraham learned to walk with God and became perfect.

When Abram was ninety-nine years old, the Lord appeared to Abram and said to him, "I am Almighty God; walk before Me and be blameless" (Genesis 17:1).

You see, a person's walk with God should progressively lead to perfection. God says, "Be ye also perfect even as your Father in heaven is" (see Matt. 5:48). If that were not possible, God would not demand it. It is possible to be perfect as one continues to walk with God.

The Bible says in Genesis 5:24: "And Enoch walked with God; and he was not, for God took him." It was the perfection of his walk with God that brought about his rapture. Today the Church is waiting for the return of the Lord in the Church to perfect her, otherwise He will not return for her. In other words, only those who will allow the Lord to return in them—in refining, in glorifying, in disciplining, in holiness, and in worship—can expect Him to return for them. Only a select few, the five wise virgins, will be able to hear the sound of the trumpet.

Then the kingdom of heaven shall be likened to ten virgins who took their lamps and went out to meet the bridegroom. Now five of them were wise, and five were foolish. Those who were foolish took their lamps and took no oil with them, but the wise took oil in their vessels with their lamps. But while the bridegroom was delayed, they all slumbered and slept. And at midnight a cry was heard: "Behold, the bridegroom is coming; go out to meet him!" Then all those virgins arose and trimmed their lamps. And the foolish said to the wise, "Give us some of your oil, for our lamps are going out." But the wise answered, saying, "No, lest there should not be enough for us and you; but go rather to those who sell, and buy for yourselves." And while they went to buy, the bridegroom came, and those who were ready went in with him to the wedding; and the door was shut. Afterward the other virgins came also, saying, "Lord, Lord, open to us!" But he answered and said, "Assuredly, I say to you, I do not know you" (Matthew 25:1-12).

For David and his men, their assignment was not complete when David became king. Until David slaughtered Amalek, he could not be king. God will not let you become king only to be slaughtered by the enemy you have not killed.

Amalek had to go. It was the beginning of the fulfillment of a greater part of the word God gave David. They still had the Philistines, the enemies within, even Absalom and the Jebusites who dwelt in the holy hill of Zion.

Jehovah said to Adonai: "Sit at My right hand, till I make *Your* enemies *Your* footstool" (Ps. 110:1). Sometimes we think once the promise has been fulfilled—"You will be king over Israel"— we have arrived. But what was at the back of God's mind for choosing David as king over Israel? Definitely there were other things, not just David's comfort and prosperity which were just a fragmented part.

Until we come to understand that the purposes of God are way beyond our comforts and prosperity, we will never be able to arrive at the ultimate destiny. David, in the sphere of God's eternal plans, will be the eternal ruler of Jerusalem. It is forever the city of David.

I do not wish to be involved in the politics of Israel and Palestine, but one thing I can say is that Jerusalem will be the eternal capital of Israel, indivisible, and there is no force on the earth that can change that. We need to know that this matter is coming from the Creator of the entire universe, and what He says no man can change. Politicians may try, but God says, "I will make Jerusalem a burdensome stone and all that burden themselves with it shall be wounded."

"And it shall happen in that day that I will make Jerusalem a very heavy stone for all peoples; all who would heave it away will surely be cut in pieces, though all nations of the earth are gathered against it" (Zech. 12:3). Some people take the Word of God and begin to play around with it. But hey! The whole world was created by God's word, and still today is upheld by the same. The word is God and is eternal. Nothing temporal can change the eternal. It is the eternal that has the ability to change the temporal.

There was a long war between the house of Saul and the house of David. David had become king, but God had something else in mind, and David had a mission to accomplish. God had a perfect Church in mind. You need to know that David is a type of the overcomer's Church, and once all the dust settles the temple must be built. The temple of God must be built on Mount Zion (Moriah), a place of the ultimate sacrifice, but no one in Israel had ever dared to dispossess the Jebusites of their domain. They lived there and were ready to stay there until someone challenged them and was willing to take them on in battle.

Taking Strongholds

There is a place in your life as a Christian that is like the stronghold of the Jebusites. It has defied all forms of appeals, prayers, or negotiations. You need to understand that only a confrontation will bring the comfort you need. You and I are the temple of God, but we must be built in conformity with the highest standards and character of God or His presence will not abide within. The good news is that He will be there to assist you in your battle.

So after David reigned in Hebron for seven years and six months, he and his men went to Jerusalem against the Jebusites, who had said that even the lame and the blind amongst them would prevent him. They thought David could not get in there.

> *And the king and his men went to Jerusalem against the Jebusites, the inhabitants of the land, who spoke to David, saying, "You shall not come in here; but the blind and the lame will repel you," thinking, "David cannot come in here"* (2 Samuel 5:6).

Nevertheless, David took that stronghold of Zion and called it the city of David, and he destroyed the lame and the blind. To take the stronghold of the enemy in any areas of your life, you have to detest all of your limitations (lameness and blindness). Your soul must hate them and not excuse them. Do not ever explain away any limitations. "Oh! I do not have money; the economy is bad; oh, I did not go to school." Those are lame excuses that the enemy will make you agree with to limit and impoverish you. Do not buy them. He (satan) is a liar and the father of all liars.

Until you dispossess him from having a stronghold in your life, the temple of God cannot be built and the glory of God will not be revealed. Once the stronghold of the Jebusites was taken, David realized the ark of God was missing. The Jebusites blind you to the most important issues of the Kingdom and continue to engage you in trivial matters. What is most important is the presence of the Lord that will ensure the ultimate victories of your kingship.

So David said, "Now that I have taken over Zion, I can get the ark," and he set out to do that. Our greatest search in this generation should not be for fame or wealth but the presence of God.

David had a good idea, but his idea was not backed up with knowledge. The lack of knowledge of the principles of God brought death to Uzzah. David and Israel put the ark on a new cart, the Philistine way, and it worked for a while.

We are not told that anyone died when the Philistines put the ark on the cart, but when the people of God did the things of God with the standard procedure of the world, God spoke out, and loudly. In other words, God can permit the world to escape in certain things, but His people who ought to know and teach the world must be corrected.

God is trying to correct the world's perception of Him and His holy standards, but His people are the instruments He will use. And if God cannot correct His own, He cannot correct the world. Judgment must start in the house of God.

So when Uzzah died, David went to search and inquired and found out that the ark was never to be put on a cart, but was to be carried by the priests. We are living in a day when the church has borrowed so much from the world. The world has become "churchy" and the church, worldly. There's so much mixture, and it is now fashionable to belong to church. That way no one suspects your dubiousness. The church provides the covering through which men can be extremely wicked and yet be seen as godly. Hypocrisy has always been and will forever be an abomination in the eyes of God.

But all of that will change, because God is in His temple as a Refiner and will thoroughly purify His Church. Nowadays, it is fashionable for church leaders to celebrate and glorify the Achans, the Ananias, and the Saphirras of the twenty-first century instead of declaring judgment. But wait a little, just a little while, and the party is about to end. When men start to die, the attention of the leaders will be caught, and they will go back to the drawing board to discover the most important things of the Kingdom—faith, mercy, and character.

David learned his lesson, and eventually the ark was brought back to the city of David. David danced before the Lord, and Saul's daughter, Michal, despised him. Saul's daughter represents the church without intimacy with Jehovah—those who cannot feel His heartbeat and will never produce purpose. There are so many

Michals who are despising David. But how did David marry Michal? Saul gave her as a snare, and David killed two hundred Philistines for her sake.

Take a moment and consider this—anything that you get because of your desire to please people will ultimately become a snare and despise you. Michal was a snare, and until David saw her for who she was and disassociated or stopped any form of intimacy, anything she could have given birth to would remain anti-purposeful. Antichrist is anything birthed by the flesh; it will persecute the spirit.

Housing His Presence

We can see a pattern in Isaac and Ishmael. Until Ishmael was cast out, Isaac would not fully inherit. Your purpose will not fully develop and become manifest as long as you're still having intimacy with the flesh and acting by the impulses of the same.

So the ark rested in the place prepared. But it still was a tent. Understand that the ultimate desire of God is not erecting a tent that can be moved from place to place. He does not want His presence to come and go. His glory may come down, be lifted up, come down again, and be lifted again, but He wants His presence to abide.

God is looking for a permanent structure that will contain the abiding presence. But God Almighty never asked anyone to build a temple up to that time. Think on this for a moment—there are so many things that God desires, but it will take a man who can access the mind of God to fish out those innermost desires and make himself available for God's use to fulfill them. A selfish man cannot see into the inner recesses of God's mind, because he has no capacity to fulfill it. God will never reveal what you have no capacity to fulfill.

It takes a selfless person to access that place in God. God may not really ask you or me to do anything, but He just wants to see how willing and how selfless we can be. If you are willing and obedient—which takes self-denial—you will eat the good of the land. God is fixing to prosper us beyond the scope of our imagination, but we need to be selfless enough to say, "God, I will build You a temple."

David purposed in his heart; he had intimacy with Jehovah, he knew God desired His presence to abide, and he said, "God, I make myself available." God's response was, "David, for just thinking about that—for accessing My thoughts—I will build you an eternal dynasty. Just for the thought, I will bless you," and He did.

David got all the plans, the design, and the prosperity and left them for Solomon, his son, to do the actual building, because God asked him not to. I guess there was only one reason why David was forbidden by God to build the temple—because of the murder of Uriah. But for the thought he got all the provision. How did David get all those provisions? Through conquest.

The Bible records that King David dedicated to the Lord the silver and gold from all the nations he subdued. He got tributes from all the nations, but he understood the reason for the prosperity.

Many times, God's people have turned to worship the gold and silver God has brought for the temple by answering to the desires of the wealth instead of the desires of God. They make a golden calf out of the silver and gold and bow down to it. God never intended us to make the pursuit of money our prime focus in life, so He made the people lay money at the feet of the apostles. The apostle is one sent out on a mission, and every time you enter your mission God brings provision, and the money is for you to walk upon and control, not for it to control you.

Do you not know that you become the servant of whatever you yield yourself to? God says He wants our undivided service and attention, so you cannot serve Him and mammon (money), but surely you have to serve Him with mammon. The jealousy of God cannot endure divided allegiance.

Israel did not leave Egypt empty-handed; they left rich, because God had the building of the tabernacle in mind. He made sure the Egyptians gave them 430 years' worth of salaries in one night. Figure that out. God will bring instantaneous prosperity to His people. He says the day I turn your captivity, you shall be like them who dream (see Ps. 126:1).

But why does He want to turn the captivity of His people? So we can return and build up Zion for God to appear in glory and power. For out of Zion, the perfection of beauty, God will shine.

Understand that your prosperity is not for personal consumption, or you will soon die of wealth suffocation and intoxication, or at worse you will grossly limit what God would have done through you. The Bible says the bloody and deceitful men will not live out half their days. So understand the purpose, for a man of understanding is of an excellent spirit (see Ps. 55:23).

God said David was a man after God's heart, and David lived out that testimony. He was always running to know the mind of God. He wrote in Psalm 42:1: "As the deer pants for the water brooks, so pants my soul for You, O God." He was a God-seeker and indeed a worshiper. Anywhere you find true seekers, you find true worshipers. There is no compulsion to becoming a true worshiper. When you seek Him diligently and are found in Him, then the overflow of worship from your heart is obvious. Until the temple implements are put in place and the temple built, true worship will not be found, and therefore an abiding glory cannot come.

When Solomon built the temple and dedicated it, glory filled the house and no flesh could stand. We are living in a day when God wants His glory to cover the earth as the waters cover the seas and abide in people—people who will contend with the Ziphites, Amalekites, Philistines, and the Jebusites.

David had to finish the battle on the plains and the valley. Any low self-esteem, insecurity, and inferiority complex will never allow you to get to the mount of the Jebusite. If you run with footmen and they weary you, how can you run with horses?

Points to Ponder

1. The battle today can only be won by the corporate Church. The days of the one man show are over.
2. God will use ordinary people who are submitted to spiritual oversight and the disciplines involved.
3. Every Christian who will ultimately enter His promise will have a wilderness experience, and your attitude will determine whether you will die there or make it to the throne.
4. God has an order, and the Church must follow due order in all she does.
5. Only selfless people will arrive at their destination.

Endnote

1. *Dictionary.com*, s.v. "Ichabod," accessed March 27, 2011, http://dictionary.reference.com/browse/ichabod.

Chapter 6

Nehemiah: The Passion for Revival

Nehemiah: The Passion for Revival

Nehemiah was a very comfortable man in Shushan (Persia). He went as a slave, but God had a plan. In Shushan, he was the king's cupbearer, but he never lost sight of the fact that he was not a Babylonian. Sometimes, when God raises His people from slavery to rulership, be it in the economic, military, or political realm, they soon forget and begin to adapt to the culture of their environment and become indifferent to the things of God.

But not Nehemiah. He constantly inquired of the state of affairs in Zion, and when he got the evil report that the walls of Jerusalem were broken down and the gates burned with fire and the people lived in penury, he forgot all his comfort and position and took a fast to seek the face of the Lord. And God gave him an answer: "Ask the king to grant you leave of absence, go back to Jerusalem and begin reconstruction" (Neh. 1:5-6 paraphrased). God backed him up, and he got more favor than he would normally have. Every time we make the work of building the Kingdom of God our concern, God makes people favor us, including kings. Our primary obligation is to ensure that the Kingdom of God prospers. If the Kingdom prospers, you will certainly prosper.

Nehemiah understood that as long as the walls of Jerusalem were broken down and the gates destroyed, just anything could access her and defile her. So are our lives; if we do not build up the broken-down walls of our lives through fasting, prayer, and our obedient walk, we cannot expect to experience the fullness of God's glory or inheritance. God will allow you to start a walk with Him as you are, but will not permit you to remain the same over time. He will not continue to put His glory on you if there is no attempt on your part to be like Him. Think in this way. You cannot begin to furnish a building that is not completed—with no windows, no roofs, and no doors—with the best kind of furniture and even add air conditioning units. That is illogical, and so also will God not pour out His glory into vessels that cannot carry it. Let me say here that there will be oppositions against you when you begin to realize that the walls of your life need rebuilding, reinforcements, and security checks.

Facing the Enemy

Nehemiah faced three vicious enemies who arose with different strategies at different times—Samballat, Tobiah, and Geshem. First it was the strategy of compromise. They said, "We will build with you."

He said, "No, you cannot, because you are not part of us" (see Neh. 2:20). Anything that is not aligned with the character and purpose of God is an enemy. It will eventually turn against you or betray you to the enemy. Compromise is one strategy that satan will always use. It will say to you, "It really doesn't matter, just do it this way; it's not that bad after all; you are not harming anyone directly, just do it your way." The Hebrew boys were tempted to compromise on their God's prescribed diets in Babylon, but they refused. Had they been defiled, they would have no strength to defy Nebuchadnezzar's image. Once defiled, you cannot defy the enemy. For the believer, God has prescribed diets. There are things you do not eat. Your appetites must change, lustful desires must die, and fleshly appetites must be killed if you are to stand in this evil day.

The enemy's next strategy was rage and ridicule.

> *But it so happened, when Sanballat heard that we were rebuilding the wall, that he was furious and very indignant, and mocked the Jews. And he spoke before his brethren and the army of Samaria, and said, "What are these feeble Jews doing? Will they fortify themselves? Will they offer sacrifices? Will they complete it in a day? Will they revive the stones from the heaps of rubbish—stones that are burned?" Now Tobiah the Ammonite was beside him, and he said, "Whatever they build, if even a fox goes up on it, he will break down their stone wall"* (Nehemiah 4:1-3).

Every time God begins to do a great work, He will use the base, despised, and foolish things. If you do not have confidence in your God-given vision and the God of the vision, you easily give up because of ridicule. I have had someone say to me, "What kind of church are you pastoring? Everything is like child's play." I wasn't bothered, because in the integrity of my heart I was doing what I knew to do under God at that time and God was with me. The strategy of ridicule is to make you lose self-worth and doubt whether God called you to do what you are doing or not. Let me say that whatever God has called you to do is not primarily about you but about Him and His people.

God has more confidence in His ability to finish His work than in your ability to mess it up. So when the enemy comes to make you see your work as a mess and a waste of time, do what Nehemiah did. "Hear, O our God, for we are despised; turn their reproach on their own heads, and give them as plunder to a land of captivity!" (Neh. 4:4). Keep praying and continue in spite of any distraction.

The next attack was a plot to come in stealthily and stop the work, but Nehemiah also developed his defense. Do not be reactive but proactive. He never reacted to the enemy's schemes but created his own. To be reactive puts you on the defensive, but to be proactive keeps you on the offensive and alert. He made sure the people stayed close enough to each other and each builder had a weapon to use in case of attack.

In the days that we are living, to be an effective builder of the Kingdom you also must be an effective warrior. You will succeed in building nothing if you do not learn to keep the enemy at bay.

> *And our adversaries said, "They will neither know nor see anything, till we come into their midst and kill them and cause the work to cease." So it was, when the Jews who dwelt near them came, that they told us ten times, "From whatever place you turn, they will be upon us." Therefore I positioned men behind the lower parts of the wall, at the openings; and I set the people according to their families, with their swords, their spears, and their bows. And I looked, and arose and said to the nobles, to the leaders, and to the rest of the people, "Do not be afraid of them. Remember the Lord, great and awesome, and fight for your brethren, your sons, your daughters, your wives, and your houses." And it happened, when our enemies heard that it was known to us, and that God had brought their plot to nothing, that all of us returned to the wall, everyone to his work. So it was, from that time on, that half of my servants worked at construction, while the other half held the spears, the shields, the bows, and wore armor; and the leaders were behind all the house of Judah. Those who built on the wall, and those who carried burdens, loaded themselves so that with one hand they worked at construction, and with the other held a weapon. Every one of the builders had his sword girded at his side as he built. And the one who sounded the trumpet was beside me* (Nehemiah 4:11-18).

Their personal comfort became inconsequential in the light of the greater purpose. Sometimes we do not really come to grips with the most important things in life, and we allow the enemy to distract us with all kinds of private agendas. When push comes to shove, some things we thought were so important and inevitable for us suddenly lose their sense and meaning.

In the face of reality, they knew that even taking their bath was a luxury they couldn't afford at the time. Once I had to visit a morgue, and the sight of men and women thrown on the bare floor of the morgue, naked and unashamed, brought to me the stark reality that life has no meaning without purpose. Purpose is the only thing you leave the world with. Let me say to you—ask yourself, "Am I living a purpose-driven life or a purposeless one?" And be quick to bow your head and ask God to tell you why He created you. Your greatest tragedy is not death, but not knowing why you are alive.

You are created to impact creation. Find out before you depart this planet. As a matter of fact, you will live forever somewhere after you have left this planet, but where and how you live is going to be determined by how purposeful or purposeless your life has been.

When the strategy of ridicule failed, they manufactured falsehood against Nehemiah.

> *Now it happened when Sanballat, Tobiah, Geshem the Arab, and the rest of our enemies heard that I had rebuilt the wall, and that there were no breaks left in it (though at that time I had not hung the doors in the gates)* (Nehemiah 6:1).

Nehemiah was a man of prayer and by implication a man of discernment, and he could see through their plans. Eventually, they hired Shemaiah to prophecy lies to frighten Nehemiah, but this also could not work because of prayers and discernment.

One of the greatest strategies that satan is using today is that of deception. Deception is a spirit released upon the world to give a false sense of security, peace, and assurance so the world can continue in their wickedness. And unfortunately many believers are buying into that same spirit because they have refused to live by the truth of God's Word.

God said:

> And with all unrighteous deception among those who perish, because they did not receive the love of the truth, that they might be saved. And for this reason God will send them strong delusion, that they should believe the lie, that they all may be condemned who did not believe the truth but had pleasure in unrighteousness (2 Thessalonians 2:10-12).

Anyone who has built into his life a culture of deception can never escape the wiles of satan. When the disciples asked Jesus what were the signs of His return, He started by saying, "Let no man deceive you" (Matt. 24:4). Deception is one of the greatest signs that we are living in the last days. These days, the difference between truth and a lie is a very thin line, and only the most discerning can escape. I happened to be in a church meeting when a "man of God" was ministering. My spirit just could not accept what he was saying, but every other person in that hall was shouting and jumping exhilaratingly. I felt like a fish out of the water, but I had learned to follow the Holy Ghost within me and I knew I was hearing God clearly. "This is fake." If you were to go by the "anointing" in the air, you would be easily deceived, which was why all my brethren there were taken in. It was a trick, but what qualifies an anointing as false or true is not the anointing but the man. Indeed, it is the character of the man. Later on, I came to know that the man was a serious "419" (a dubious character) and also involved in immoral acts. That concluded my reservation and inability to open my spirit for his ministration. The letters of his words were true, but the spirit of his word was fake. You have to go past the letter of the word today and look at the spirit behind it if you wish to escape deception.

Nehemiah did just that. Eventually the work was finished and God was glorified. Whenever you begin an assignment of reconstruction, God will help you to finish the work if you refuse to buy into the strategies and deception of satan and his cohorts. No weapon formed against you will prosper, and when they come against you one way, they will flee in seven (see Isa. 54:17 and Deut. 28:7). God will make you a brazen pillar and defense wall; they will come against you but will never prevail against you.

Points to Ponder

1. Passion for God must overwhelm personal comfort or you will not go far for Him in these days.
2. Do not wait for everyone to understand what God has told you. Just start, and He will raise people to help you fulfill the vision.
3. Enemies will come with ridicule, compromise, lies, threats, and intimidation. Fear none of these things.
4. Rid yourself of double standards and deception.
5. God will finish the work.

Chapter 7

Esther: Dying to Self: A Key to Breaking Ground for Victory

Esther: Dying to Self: A Key to Breaking Ground for Victory

Esther began her life as an orphan adopted by Mordecai, her uncle, but through the providence of God she found herself as the Queen of Persia. Let me say you—your present position in life is not an indicator of how you will end. Odds may be against you, but the purpose of God will bring you to fame and prominence. God is sovereign.

Now Esther had a choice—to remain queen and be comfortable in the palace, or to rise up for her people. She chose the latter in spite of the fact that her personal safety and comfort were in jeopardy. How far can we go to see that God's Kingdom and people are not exterminated by poverty and diseases?

How much of our personal pride, prejudice, security, and safety can we jeopardize to see God's glory revealed? Esther said, "If I perish, I perish" (Esther 4:16). Until the Church rises up to jeopardize our personal comforts—ego, material things, denominational barriers, doctrines, wrong perceptions, and emphases—we will allow the enemy to continue to wipe out God's people and indeed God's purpose.

Esther represents the ultimate Church who will love not their lives unto death so that the will of God will be established on the earth. Now, you need to know that Esther was sovereignly brought into the palace for the need of that hour—the salvation of the Jews. Once you understand why God has saved you in this time and has singled you out, then you can indeed channel your resources to the expansion of His Kingdom.

One of the weapons that God has equipped the Church with is fasting and prayer. Esther fasted and prayed, and God began to move behind the scenes and brought her favor with the king. Favor is what every believer needs in these last days. God has great plans for His people, but without favor our labor will be in vain. No amount of human labor can bring the Church to the place of that ultimate wealth and glory.

Esther became queen. I guess that would have been enough for any purposeless person to say, "I have arrived." But wait! The position of queen is only a means to an end, never the end in itself. Perhaps we should ask ourselves over and over again the reasons behind the mercy, favor, and faithfulness of God toward us.

God is purpose-oriented; in other words, He does everything with a purpose in mind. So if Esther just became queen and never pursued the salvation of her people, purpose would be defeated.

I would like to examine the key players in this book.

Vashti

Vashti represents those in the church who have refused to submit to the lordship of the King and Lord. They have refused to display the beauty of the King for the people.

Now, we are born again to display the awesome majesty of God on the earth, but without the formation and display of God's character, we cannot show the world how great God is. So the emphasis of God in these last days is the formation of character, indeed, the display of the love of God which manifests in joy, peace, longsuffering, gentleness, goodness, faithfulness, and patience. In short, the fruit of the Spirit.

But the fruit of the Spirit is love, joy, peace, longsuffering, kindness, goodness, faithfulness (Galatians 5:22).

Therefore by their fruits you will know them (Matthew 7:20).

Vashti does not qualify for this present move of God and she has to be replaced by Esther. Now Esther, you need to know that it was not your beauty that got you here; it was not your intellectual capabilities; it was simply God's favor. There are Esthers replacing Vashtis now as there are Davids replacing the Sauls. The latter must render all due honor and respect, pondering and contemplating on the purpose that brought them to prominence in the first place.

Mordecai

He was a Jew, a Jew indeed, refusing to compromise and bow to Haman. Sometimes when Christians find themselves in worldly circles, they begin to bend and compromise for what their bellies stand to benefit. But here was a Jew who held the laws of Jehovah above his personal gains and comforts, and in so doing jeopardized the lives of all the Jews.

One could say Mordecai lacked wisdom; he should have bowed to Haman. After all, it wouldn't hurt anyone, right? No, it would hurt Jehovah, who had decreed that His people would not bow themselves to anyone but Himself. Jehovah was well able to defend His people, and He did.

Often, when believers refuse to compromise, the enemy begins a cycle of afflictions, torments, and persecutions, but God will always defend the cause of the righteous. The Bible says a lying tongue is for a moment (see Prov. 12:19). So truth will always prevail, evil will always bow before good, and light will always overcome darkness. This is the assurance that we have.

These things I have spoken to you, that in Me you may have peace. In the world you will have tribulation; but be of good cheer, I have overcome the world (John 16:33).

Haman prepared the gallows for Mordecai, but he was hanged on it. What the enemy plans to use against you will be same thing God will use to kill him. Sometime before, Mordecai had done a great favor for the king warranting a reward, but nothing was done for him. Here is a lesson: God will delay some rewards until the time of your need. The night Haman planned to hang Mordecai, the king could not sleep. You see, one good turn deserves another. Whatever you have personally sown will assuredly come back to you as a harvest, either good or bad.

Mordecai saved the king's life and the king, by the law of reciprocity, saved Mordecai's life. Had Mordecai been rewarded when the deed was done, he would not have had any reward left for the greatest hour of his need.

Do not be quick to complain about not getting a reward for your good deeds, because you will surely get it at your greatest hour of need. Perhaps even your posterity will come to enjoy the reward of your good deeds.

We can see this clearly in the people of the United States of America. Their forefathers left a lasting legacy of godly deeds so their children after them, in spite of their present perversions, are still enjoying the rewards. What nation on earth has spread the Gospel the way they have, what nation has given the way they have, and what nation is as blessed as they are? Good seeds—good harvests.

When the records were brought to the king and he saw that Mordecai had never been rewarded for saving his life, he instantly—I believe by the prompting of the divine hand—proposed to reward Mordecai. What a timely intervention. We are living in a time when God will work tirelessly behind the scenes to bring His people out of destruction and from death to life and wealth.

This is the time when the world says, "It is finished with you," and suddenly the tables are turned against them. A time when one night you are in the slums and the next day in the capitol. When all you knew the day before was shame and sorrow, and within twelve hours you have fame and glory. It is a time when your enemies will be the ones to parade you to glory. Oh, what a time for God's people! There will be no time like it again.

So Church, put on your armor of strength, defy every odd in your life, defy death, defy satan, defy lack, defy sickness, defy diseases, and rise to power, glory, and fame.

Mordecai in one night took possession of Haman's wealth, position, and glory. Oh, I feel like jumping, because I can see the Church that will dispossess the world of their ill-gotten wealth and sanctify it to the King of kings and Lord of lords. A Church that will strip the devil of the armors in which he trusted in times past and sanctify them to our God. A glorious, powerful, wealthy, and invincible Church, halleluiah!

Issues of the Corporate Church

Esther and Mordecai played their individual roles successfully, but it will take all the Jews in the kingdom to deal with the residual resistance. I have always known that the word will come to one, but it will take a company to possess it. The word of promise is far too big for any one person to possess. The corporate Church will stand to benefit if the leadership begins to deemphasize themselves and allow the Church to pay attention to the Master Himself.

In other words, each saint should be taught to work out his salvation with fear and trembling. The situation where the saints depend on pastors or evangelists (leadership) for all their needs is completely unacceptable in this hour. Each must learn to deal with the enemy and defeat him in conjunction with the Holy Spirit within them. God's will is to have a Body of people who will arise wherever they are to contend with the enemies that will seek to exterminate them.

Something I need to mention here is the fact that the decree that was sent through Haman was not repealed. So Esther and Mordecai had to write a higher decree. In this final hour, we need to put a higher law in force if we are to overcome the law of sin and death; this is the law of the spirit of life in Christ Jesus (see Rom. 8:2). Just like the law or principle of lift is what enables the aircraft to overcome the law of gravity, so also the saints must operate in this higher law if we intend to deal with all enemies.

The ultimate warrior needs to be skillful in spiritual warfare and recognize that only the principles of the Word of God can guarantee their victory. So the Jews had rest and gladness of heart. Again we see that it took Esther's and Mordecai's actions for all the Jews to have rest in the land. Oh, the wisdom of God. The saints need the leadership and the leadership in turn needs the saints if purpose will be actualized. For God has given apostles, prophets, teachers, pastors, and evangelists for the equipping of the saints, so the saints can do the work of the ministry, and so the Body can be edified and God will be glorified (see Eph. 4:11).

Points to Ponder

1. Those in the church who refuse to obey instructions that will show forth God's glory on the earth are now being dethroned like Vashti. Obey the King's instructions.

2. Die to self. That is the only way to truly live now.

3. Do not make excuses; even if you are in comfort you may not survive.

4. Stay under leadership and you will fulfill your ultimate destiny.
5. Remember, getting to the throne was a means to an end, not an end in itself.

Chapter 8

Joshua: A Warrior With a Divine Vision

Joshua: A Warrior With a Divine Vision

Not much was said about Joshua's beginning except that he was the son of Nun and he was Moses' servant. And that, to my mind, is a good beginning as we consider the word servant.

A servant is one who serves. He or she takes care of the welfare of another person. Joshua was faithful, and so when Moses was old and could no longer go out or come in, Joshua was then commissioned to take the people across the Jordan to the Promised Land.

> *And he said to them: "I am one hundred and twenty years old today. I can no longer go out and come in. Also the Lord has said to me, 'You shall not cross over this Jordan'"* (Deuteronomy 31:2).

Moses was a shepherd, but Joshua was a warrior. Both ministries are needed to get the people out of Egypt to the Promised Land.

In our day and hour, the promised land is not a physical location but a place where people are completely empty of the flesh and its attitudes, ready to be filled with the fullness of God and His Divine Nature Attributes (DNA).

> *Till we all come to the unity of the faith and of the knowledge of the Son of God, to a perfect man, to the measure of the stature of the fullness of Christ* (Ephesians 4:13).

The warrior mentality in Joshua was going to be tested and proved as Israel began a phase of their lives without Moses. Sometimes when our familiars suddenly are taken away, instead of embracing the new we sit and mourn and desire the past. So God came to Joshua and declared, "Moses My servant is dead," emphasizing to him that the past was gone and he needed to embrace the future. "So arise" (see Josh. 1:2). I guess Joshua was in no mood to accept that Moses could die and certainly was not in any way ready to walk away from the mountains of Nebo opposite Jericho.

Sometimes we are too paralyzed by our losses to embrace our future. Jericho was right before them, but they had Jordan to conquer. I believe Israel could not fathom how they could go over the Jordan.

But when God leads you out, He will bring you in. Before time began, He had figured out how they would go over it. I need to tell you that God figured out the process of crossing the Jordan before you came out of Egypt. So rest assured in His competence, love, and wisdom. Joshua was encouraged by the Lord and commanded to be strong, vigorous, and very courageous.

Possessing the Land

It will certainly take the mindset of fearlessness to conquer the enemies in the land. Possessing the land means dispossessing the occupants, but they will put up a fight and you had better be fearless because it will be a fight to the finish. The advantage that Israel had, which the present Church also has, was the fact that God was with them, and He is also with us. The difference in any battle is simply the presence or absence of God.

If God be for us—and He is—who can be against us? So Joshua, being overwhelmed by God's favor and encouragement, took command of the people and began to advance them into their destinies. Every believer has a destiny in God, but it will take the leadership of men like Joshua to cause them to inherit their inheritance by maximizing their potential.

The Church has to understand the ministry of men like Joshua, for they have not come for a game or a show, but for serious business with God and His people.

Whenever God makes a promise, it will take the diligent, the disciplined, and the determined to access it. Joshua is always seen and heard commanding the people.

Joshua's ministry is not a ministry that comes to plead, cajole, or compromise with the people. We are living in a generation where people are plagued with itchy ears; they come to church wishing to hear what will tickle their fleshy minds and are on treadmills, running all around in circles and going nowhere in particular.

These are people who have religion and no relationship. They have the motions and not motivation. Confessions not convictions, having a form of godliness but not the power of godliness. These are people like Saul, who was head and shoulders above all but had no answer for the Philistine giants. These are men with "great visible ministries" but no inner structure to carry. These are men with "sky scrapers" but no foundation, and any little wind blowing in their direction will mess them up and blow them to pieces.

It is high time for the Church to understand that God brought us out to bring us in and it will take an army formation and mentality to dispossess the enemy of our rightful inheritance. So it is no longer "church as usual" but "church unusual."

Emerging Weapons

In Joshua 2, Joshua sent men secretly to spy the land and they found favor with Rahab. Let me say that until the Church cooperates with the Joshua style of leadership, there will be many Rahabs and families who will never realize their destinies. Rahab became the great-great-grandmother of King David, who was an ancestor of the Messiah. Did God plan this for her? Yes, of course, but it had to take the obedience of men under the leadership of Joshua to locate and connect her with her destiny.

In Joshua 3, Joshua rose early in the morning and led the whole of Israel to move from Shittim. Shittim represents a place of human settlement under fleshy calculations and permutations. As long as the people remain in Shittim, they are still a long way from their destiny.

"The carnal mind is enmity against God" (Rom. 8:7) and indeed is not subject to the law of God. To be carnally minded is death. Carnality is the destruction of the present Church. But God has a people in the midst of the Church—a "church within the Church"—who will rise up by faith and destroy every human calculation and assumption, who will defy all physical evidence before them that contradicts the Word of God, and who will quench the fire, stop the mouths of lions, and receive their dead back to life by their faith.

> *Who through faith subdued kingdoms, worked righteousness, obtained promises, stopped the mouths of lions* (Hebrews 11:33).

This generation will not end before such a church emerges. Moreover, without the emergence of this church, glorious, powerful, and wealthy Christ is not coming. We should stop to ask ourselves—did Christ die to have the church we are today? Poor, weather-beaten, downtrodden, beggarly, miserable, with no confidence, and totally incapable of doing damage to the powers of darkness? My answer is unequivocally *no!*

If all we have today was the mind of God when He sent Christ to die, then I bet He could have found another way. Christ died so that the Church that He purchased with His very blood would become the most potent tool that Jehovah has on the earth for the final assault on the kingdom of darkness.

We are to spoil the works of satan on the earth and suffocate his mission in the lives of people. But you cannot give what you don't have. If we have no victories in our lives as believers, how can we give such to the world? If we can hardly have peace ourselves, what can we share? It will take leaders with the mentality of Joshua to enable the people to cross over the Jordan.

The Bible records in Joshua 3:15:

> *And as those who bore the ark came to the Jordan, and the feet of the priests who bore the ark dipped in the edge of the water (for the Jordan overflows all its banks during the whole time of harvest)....*

We are now in the season of great harvest—financial harvest, harvest of souls, and harvest of life. But do not think the enemy will not come like a flood. Nevertheless, the Kingdom of God must advance and forceful people will lay hold of it. How then shall we know that the living God is among us unless He drives away all enemies of His purpose?

So the priests who bore the Ark of the Covenant were commanded to go before their brethren, but not until the people set out from their camp and stepped into the Jordan. I believe that in these last days, God has a company of people who will be clothed with power and presence, and those will be a breaker company of people who will make a way for others to access their purpose in God. These are the ones who will step first into the Jordan, symbolically dying to self, and remain there unshaken, insurmountable, and invincible in the face of all the overflow of iniquity until their brethren have had a clean pass into the promised land.

Oh, how excited I am writing this! Because I see that this mortal body will put on immortality and the corruptible will put on the incorruptible and death will be swallowed up in victory and the last enemy will be defeated by the glorious company about to emerge.

The Bible records that the instant the soles of the feet of the priests who bore the ark rested in the Jordan, the waters of the Jordan were cut off and stood in one heap. See! When God wants to destroy the enemy that's coming against your life like a flood, He freezes them up. One heap! The whole of the Jordan stood in one heap. Oh, what an awesome God we serve.

There, all of Israel passed over on dry ground, then Joshua told the people to make a memorial of the things that God had accomplished. He took twelve stones from where the priests had stood and he built a memorial. We need to build memorials of the faithfulness of God for the coming generations so they can serve our God.

What memorials are you laying for your children and grandchildren, even those yet unborn? Hardly are we joyful? How can we give joy to others? It is time for us to arise and fulfill our destiny by pursuing the enemies and ridding our territories of these unwanted intruders. The heavens God kept for Himself, but the earth He has given to men—His men (see Ps. 115).

I tell the church that everywhere I am is my territory. In other words, if I come to your house it is my territory and I am obligated to rid that environment of "rodents" and "insects." The believer is a spiritual pesticide and air freshener that the world needs in order to end the pollution and corruption that sin has brought. But the Church cannot rise to that level without people like Joshua who will hear from God, take the arms, and command the people.

Circumcise the Flesh

When Israel came to Gilgal, God told Joshua to make a sharp knife and circumcise the people a second time. What did God mean by this? We see that God gave the covenant of circumcision to Abraham before Isaac could come forth.

> *This is My covenant which you shall keep, between Me and you and your descendants after you: Every male child among you shall be circumcised* (Genesis 17:10).

The promises of God can never be fully apprehended while the foreskin of the flesh and heart are still standing. It has to be removed. The flesh is the greatest enemy of purpose because it has the inherent tendency to align with the enemy to abort purpose. It needs to be removed.

The foreskin of the heart will never permit the believer to be sensitive to the mind of God. The fleshy mind is calloused and will never become malleable in the hand of God. So Joshua was commanded to make a sharp knife. The sharpness of the knife will determine the efficiency and speed with which circumcision is carried out.

In the church today, we have become motivational speakers and spiritual encouragers of people who are in a terrible state of decadence and depravity. The Word of God is not coming sharply enough to rebuke, correct, and instruct people in the way of purpose and righteousness, so what we have is a church full of spiritual babies who are ever yearning for some pacifiers to shut their crying and lustful lips. But pacifiers do not have any milk—they are there to give illusion, but no substance is entering the babies, no food, no nutrients. Oh, how the church has been malnourished and reduced to being an underdog.

God is a "Jew" and He wants high yields and profitability from His people. He expects to get profits for His investments, and that rightly so. So when we fail to allow His hands to mold and make us, even cutting off excess flesh in us, our yields become very low or nonexistent and ultimately we die.

Death of purpose and destiny is the greatest tragedy that can befall a believer. Physical death is just a change of abode for the believer, but when purpose dies then that believer, even though alive, is better off physically dead. When you have no reason to live, then life itself becomes useless. What will it profit a man to gain the whole world and lose his soul? I believe losing one's soul is not necessarily going to hell, but simply the inability to fully connect with the Spirit to download the mind of God for creating you.

What did God have in mind when He formed you? When Jesus came to the earth, He located His purpose in the volume of the books.

> *Sacrifice and offering You did not desire; my ears You have opened. Burnt offering and sin offering You did not require. Then I said, "Behold, I come; in the scroll of the book it is written of me. I delight to do Your will, O my God, and Your law is within my heart"* (Psalm 40:6-8).

He went to the Book of Isaiah and read before the people His mission statement.

> *The Spirit of the Lord is upon Me, because He has anointed Me to preach the gospel to the poor; He has sent Me to heal the brokenhearted, to proclaim liberty to the captives and recovery of sight to the blind, to set at liberty those who are oppressed* (Luke 4:18).

What is your mission statement? God said to Jeremiah, "Before I formed you, I knew you and ordained you a prophet unto nations." Sometimes we are too intimidated by our weakness to lay hold of the plans of God. So God told Jeremiah not to allow his "childhood" and inability to speak to interfere with his calling. Whatever your weaknesses are, in purpose they will become your strengths. God is able to make all grace abound toward you so that in His sufficiency you can abound in every good work.

Oh, if we could truly depend on God's strength instead of looking at our weaknesses. God wants us to acknowledge our weaknesses but never use them as an excuse for our non-productivity. He is more than enough for us, and it is He who works in us to perform His good pleasures. So ultimately, it is not our strength but His.

God's Truth

When Moses sent the spies out to have an overview of the land, they all returned with the fruit of the land—beautiful. An assurance that God meant what He said to them. But the report that ten of the spies gave was evil. Now, let's ask some questions. Did they see giants in the land? Were they truthful about what they said? The answer to the first question is *yes*, but for the second, *no!*

There is a big difference between facts and truth. One's experience may be factual, but if it does not line up with God's Word, it is not the truth. The truth is God's Word. God said their report was evil because they failed to speak God's word, which is truth, but declared their experiences. Now God never said to deny our experiences, but don't allow them to lead us in making decisions or even in thinking in ways that limit God and His word to us. For this evil report, God swore they would not enter and possess the land.

The bottom line is unbelief. Many have failed to possess their possessions because of unbelief. This to me is a tool in the hands of the enemy to stop the Church from entering into great dimensions of spiritual exploits in Christ. God is not a man that He should lie or the son of man to repent; His promises are yes and amen and His word is already settled in Heaven.

We are given the privilege to enforce His Word on the earth. So no matter one's experiences, the Word of God remains faithful and God is faithful to His Word. Your experiences cannot negate the faithfulness and infallibility of God's Word, but God's Word can negate your experiences and bring them in line with the truth.

The Bible says a lying tongue is but for a moment (see Prov. 12:19); let God be true and let all experiences be found liars. Every time we make the Word of God void because of unbelief, we make God out to be a liar and it hurts His integrity exceedingly. It is extremely dangerous on our part to willingly negate God's omnipotence and sovereignty through unbelief and human reasoning.

Our human unbelief and doubts can never do away with the truth that God is all-powerful and capable of doing all He says He will do. The priests who bore the ark went before the people, and Joshua asked the people to pass over before the ark of the Lord. The ark of the Lord represents how the express presence of God was and still is the prerequisite for victory. Without the presence of the Lord going ahead of His people, there can never be victory. In Psalm 114, the psalmist recounts that it was the presence that caused the sea, the mountains, and all enemies to flee and be defeated.

It is important for this generation to learn that it is the manifest presence of God in the life of the believer that guarantees victory over the enemies. Our enemies are not physical but spiritual, and their antics can only be overcome when the presence of God fills the life of the believer to the point of directing and controlling his every thought, word, and action. Only then can the believer truly be an overcomer.

The enemies the present Church is contending with have become more and more determined in wickedness. No human calculations, reasonings, or efforts can overcome them. It will take the overflowing presence of God to dislodge them from our land.

At every step of the journey, we see Joshua commanding the priests, commanding the people. Oh, how the present Church needs the commands and disciplines it takes to get to the promised land. The present-day believers are self-destroyed; no one wants to listen to the voice of instructors. It is now fashionable to go from church to church looking for leaders who will tell them what they want to hear. Oh, how many believers will die without attempting to attain to the highest call of God for their lives?

I believe eternity will be filled with born-again believers who never lived out a fraction of their potential in God because they refused instructions and commands. They want to live their life in the fullness of lust and still access purpose. This is absolutely impossible. If it was possible to access purpose without the crucifixion of the flesh, Jesus would not have gone to the Cross. The Cross is simply an emblem of self-crucifixion, and Jesus said if anyone seeks to follow Him let him deny himself, pick up his cross, and follow. Without the carrying of your cross, you cannot follow Jesus, and without following Jesus, you can never arrive anywhere near purpose and destiny.

In other words, you are just a living dead. True life begins when the outward man is crucified with Christ. Paul said:

> *I have been crucified with Christ; it is no longer I who live, but Christ lives in me; and the life which I now live in the flesh I live by faith in the Son of God, who loved me and gave Himself for me* (Galatians 2:20).

After they had all crossed the Jordan, Joshua commanded the priests to get out of the Jordan (see Josh. 4:17). Why was this command necessary? Human nature is always comfortable in the known and familiar territories. But when God is in charge, He takes you away from the known and familiar each time He wants to take you into the next level, so men and woman like Joshua are there to see into the mind of God and command the people to get out of the familiar from time to time. Notice that God does not move you at your convenience or time but in His time and purpose. Sometimes His omniscience does not permit your timing because His perspective and overview of all events inform His very judgment at any given moment. He sees far into the future and can bring together a series of events to fulfill His purpose, and we cannot do that.

> *So it was, when all the kings of the Amorites who were on the west side of the Jordan, and all the kings of the Canaanites who were by the sea, heard that the Lord had dried up the waters of the Jordan from before the children of Israel until we had crossed over, that their heart melted; and there was no spirit in them any longer because of the children of Israel* (Joshua 5:1).

PROSPERITY

When God is responsible for the happenings in your life, all enemies will have no spirit left in them. You see, if a man makes things happen for you, men can also rise up to undo it if they choose, but no man can undo what God has done for you. No! No one can; not even the devil can.

So Jericho was shut up because of Israel; none went in and none came out. The enemies will put themselves in their self-imposed prison, but when God is ready to dispossess them, every prison gate and wall will come down.

Jericho is the city of palm and representative of prosperity. The first city the invading armies of God must endeavor to capture in this season is their prosperity for posterity. History will not forgive the present Church if we hand over poverty to our posterity.

The whole purpose of the enemy is to stop the advancement of the cities of God. God declared in Zechariah 1:17:

> *Again proclaim, saying, "Thus says the Lord of hosts: 'My cities shall again spread out through prosperity; the Lord will again comfort Zion, and will again choose Jerusalem.'"*

Let me say that the Church has wrongly presented the purpose and message of prosperity.

Prosperity is not about possessions, it is a matter that deals with purpose and destiny. Also, the possession of money is not an indicator of prosperity. Poverty is not the absence of money either, but the absence of God's wisdom, grace, and abilities that provide access for the natural man to tap into the supernatural to meet his needs and God's needs on the earth. God's needs? Yes, God's needs. God needs you and me on the earth to be the extension of His love, mercy, and help to humanity, and it will take accessing the supernatural to achieve that goal. To me, that is true prosperity.

Anything, including money, can be possessed, and that is the blessing that makes people rich and adds no sorrow (see Prov. 10:22). God's Word is clear in respect to the prosperity of His people. He created the whole world for His people, and anything that impoverishes His people in the midst of His abundant creation is certainly not His will and should be resisted as a plague.

Poverty is a plague and a mindset that has kept the Church from possessing and reaping the earth and its resources to sanctify them to our God. Jesus never meant that people who had great riches were disqualified from entering the Kingdom. If that were so, who is as rich as God Himself? He meant people who trust in their riches. It is not money that is the root of all evil, but the love of money.

> *For the love of money is a root of all kinds of evil, for which some have strayed from the faith in their greediness, and pierced themselves through with many sorrows* (1 Timothy 6:10).

One can have money and not love it. To love money is simply to allow the spirit of money to control your actions and attitudes. In other words, money should not rule your heart and life. God does not want money on your head, so the early Church laid it at the apostles' feet. On the contrary, God wants his Holy Spirit to rule your life and guide you on how you use money. The first thing that we all must agree with is that a person's life does not consist of the abundance of things he possesses. We came into this world empty, and it is obvious that we will leave with nothing.

So why do we need money? The simple truth is that money answers earthly needs, and it has a purchasing power. If God's Kingdom must advance on the earth, the Church must control the wealth and the resources of the earth. I believe the Church needs to be rich.

Now Jericho was a city with high walls. The Scriptures say, "The rich man's wealth is like a high wall in his own conceit" (see Prov. 18:11). We are to have riches but never to trust in them as our means of security and safety. God knew that the issue of Jericho was not going to be solved by Israel. The walls were too high and impenetrable, so what He did was appear to Joshua as the captain of the Lord's host. When He came, He never took sides. Joshua said, "Are you for us or for our enemies?" His reply was simply "Nay." In other words, "I am on the side of whoever conforms."

The walls of the world's economics and finances have been almost too impenetrable, and only the ungodly have had access to them for a long time. Now God wants the godly to begin to take charge, but only if they are willing to glorify God with the wealth. Do you see that wealth and money do not respond to godliness, they only respond to proper usage? In other words, money does not come to you because of who you are—only if you obey its laws. This is another topic for another book. The laws of money demand wisdom, creativity, and proper management for growth. And unfortunately, most believers lack all those things. It took skillfulness and prudence on the part of Joseph to store up harvests for the time of famine. So the captain of the Lord's host literally said, "I am not coming to give you prosperity just because you are called by My name. I can turn and give to the enemies, or whoever will respond to My needs. I will give you Jericho; I have brought you so far, but the way you act from now on will determine whether you can handle true riches."

So Joshua's first instruction was, "Take off your shoes; you are standing on holy ground" (see Josh. 5:15). In other words, "Joshua, you must now be very sensitive to the things that I will command you to do in and around Jericho (your prosperity)." A man who is walking on bare feet will be extremely cautious of where he puts his feet. The leadership of the Church should know that the tithes and the offerings are holy ground, and therefore they should receive instructions for disbursements. Presumption is a sin punishable by death, and God has never changed.

God does not need money in Heaven, but He knows its importance on the earth. His major concern when He brings money is the welfare of His people. People are His major concern on the earth. The wealth should build people and not palaces. I believe that God's people will own houses they did not build and drive cars they did not buy, but the focus of the leaders should be to help the people with the wealth.

Anything you do as a leader must be focused on changing the lot of the people. Sadly, the leadership today often think that it is the lot of the people to change their status. I totally disagree with that arrangement. Surely God will use the people, but what has the leader deposited in them? If you have no deposit and you attempt to draw from the account, you are a fraud.

There are many fraudsters in ministry defrauding the people, milking and fleecing the sheep and leaving them "naked" and drained to face the harsh weather of life. Let me say to such leadership—your days of rulership are over. God has always been and will always be careful about the well-being of His people—spiritually, emotionally, financially, and materially. When the leaders preach to the people to give, do they lead by example? Any leader who cannot shoulder the needs of his ministry under God should never expect much from the people. Leaders must lead by example. Before I ask the church for an offering for any project, I first go to God to settle the matter and ask Him how much I personally should do in the matter.

God told me to first prevail with Him before I prevail with men. "What you have not spoken to Me about, do not attempt to get it from men; if you do, you will fail." So I pray without ceasing, and by the time I make a demand the earth will only be responding to Heaven's decree.

Obeying God

The Bible records that when Jacob heard that Esau was coming against him with four hundred men, he first began with human calculation, reasoning, and manipulation. He divided his family into groups and placed Rachel and Joseph last. In other words, Esau could kill all others as long as Rachel and Joseph were spared. I am convinced that God spoke to him that "by strength shall no man prevail," and he quickly sent everyone away from him and settled down to settle issues with God—*all alone.*

Esau represents the things from our pasts that are trying to impede our journey into the future. The wars that our parents and even we fought and ran away from. But until Jacob prevailed with God and became a prince of God, he could not tackle Esau. When Jacob prevailed with God, everything, including Esau, became at peace with him.

When a man's ways please the Lord, He makes even his enemies to be at peace with him (Proverbs 16:7).

See, the issue was not even about Esau—it was all about Jacob. There was too much of "Jacob" (whose name means "trickster, fraud, manipulation") in Jacob, and God had to deal with that.

When God asked Jacob his name for the first time in his life, he whispered—in utter shock and disbelief—a name that he knew was overdue for change. A new name is always a reward for those who have prevailed and overcome. As you are reading this book, I sense in my spirit that the time has come for you to have a new name. I do not know what name men called you; but in Jesus' name, if you have read this book up to this point now, you have a heart for God and your reward is a new name.

Joshua obeyed. A leadership that does not obey God will die with all their followership in the sea of mediocrity, obscurity, and poverty. Oh, I can hear some people say, "But we are rich even though we have not obeyed God, or we even know some leaders who are living in sin and disobedience and they are rich." Do not be deceived. The prosperity of fools will destroy them, and very soon.

A false sense of security is what they have, and the Bible says that because they choose not to believe the truth of God's Word they will be punished (see 2 Thess. 1:8-9). God Himself gave them a spirit of delusion. They flatter and deceive themselves in their eyes until their iniquity swallows and ensnares them.

When Ahab decided that the prophet Micaiah was too radically against him, God permitted a lying spirit into the mouth of all his prophets and they told him what he wanted to hear (see 1 Kings 22:6). It took Micaiah to discern to truth of the situation.

There are people who can still hear God today in the midst of all the jamboree called church meetings and all the confusions of men called leaders of church. Indeed, I believe the true leaders of the church are being incubated in the womb of the Spirit of God, and suddenly God will show them to the world. There is too much noise right now, but God is looking for a voice. You can be one. You do not need to be a son of a prophet. All the sons of the prophets were too lethargic to follow Elijah. They knew the timings and the seasons of God's move. They prophesied, but they stayed behind. There is a company of people who have been left behind right now, and when Elisha returns after seeing Elijah off and crossing the Jordan twice, he will come to be their leader. They shall come begging him to heal their lands. Oh, what a tragedy for compromised, complacent, and lethargic leadership.

They have failed God and indeed failed their generations. Did God know they would fail? Did He make a contingent plan? Yes. You who are now reading this book are part of the contingent plan. Fix yourself in His purpose. The things God is about to do now are with no-name preachers. The "big men of God" are almost bigger than God Himself, and you can quote me.

We have a precedent in Saul. He started humbly, but fame and position entered his head and he became too busy to seek God and hear God for himself. He began to busy himself with the pursuit of David instead of the pursuit of God. Whenever focus is taken from God and placed on ministry, people, and things, purpose dies. Whenever there is a death of purpose, the man ceases to be useful to God and men, and it will only be a matter of time before his ultimate exit from public view and function.

God has no investments now for purposeless leadership. Moreover, the seventh trumpet is sounding now, and God is just waiting for David to be ready to recover all from the Amalekites at Ziglag before announcing the old prophets' formal exit from offices.

You may ask how I know all this. You see, the realm of the spirit determines what you see, so I keep myself pure and holy and I can see into the mind of God with clarity of vision. Once your heavens are opened, you can see visions of God. The problem with most leadership is that the heavens are closed over them. If you as a leader do not tithe, your heavens will be closed. God and His Word respect no positions. They respect obedience.

Jericho gave in to God's order and instructions at the arrival and obedience of God's people. Your present Jericho will certainly collapse as you march before it in complete obedience and submission. The Word of God records that when your obedience is fully complete and secure, all disobedience shall be avenged.

The lesson that God is giving this present Church—the same one He gave to the Israelites in the wilderness—is "touch not the devoted things." As there were in those days, there are things in the present-day Church that are to be completely burned in the fire of God's wrath. Disobedience then brought death and defeat. So it is now. Achan the son of Carmi brought defeat to the camp.

> *But the children of Israel committed a trespass regarding the accursed things, for Achan the son of Carmi, the son of Zabdi, the son of Zerah, of the tribe of Judah, took of the accursed things; so the anger of the Lord burned against the children of Israel* (Joshua 7:1).

In the present Church, there are many Achans who are being celebrated by church leaders even though defeat abounds everywhere in the church. The pastors have ceased to be spiritually sensitive. Church members are dying, committing abominable sins, having no spiritual victory, losing daily battles of life, and living completely compromised lifestyles.

God's judgment is coming in limited measures, and still the Achans are celebrated. People in church are sick, and some are dying. Even ministers and congregations have had to bury very young pastors. This to my mind is a wake-up call from Heaven. All is not well with the Church. But as a prophet of God, I declare that it will not be business as usual for the Church and her leadership. God is changing all that. The Achans who have steadily brought defeat and decay to the entire Body of Christ will begin to die for their sins. There will be a falling away and a cutting away before Christ returns to the earth.

Coming Again

Now talking about the return of the Messiah, even the dullest of the people spiritually can see that everything in the world is failing and there are no logical explanations. Politicians are failing in all of their attempts to broker peace in the most volatile regions of the earth. Wars and rumors of wars, earthquakes and tsunamis, heat waves and signs—God will show the complacent Church that Jesus is coming, and very soon (see Matt. 24).

Thank God for Joshua's type of leadership—those who can fall face down before God and seek answers. When Achan died, victory returned. Perhaps you are sensing defeat in areas of your life. Fall face down before God and ask Him to reveal any "Achan" in your camp. If the devil has no foothold in your life, he cannot dig a hole for your life. Clear every Achan out of the way and begin to enjoy the victories of the day.

I charge every pastor to look critically into themselves and their congregations and ask the Holy Spirit to forcibly remove every Achan, because until Achan leaves you can experience no victories. This is not to witch hunt or suspect people. This is a matter of falling before God, asking for Him to forcibly remove things in you or even people who are linked to you who will never allow you to have victory in your ministries.

For a very long time, I had "good" people who just would not allow the fullness of God in them, so they constituted spiritual blockades to the purposes of God. Except for a few cases, I have never personally sent anyone out of the church. They go because I prayed, and that prayer was not directed at them. But because they would not yield to purpose and my prayer was about purpose, all anti-purpose persons and stuff had to go. God is not as concerned with the comforts of individuals as He is with purpose. If you are on the side of purpose, you go forward; on the wrong side of purpose, you get excavated out.

I always remind people that life or death is simply an issue of purpose. For purpose Christ died. God will do away with the good to establish the best. It is always better to allow Him to work out His purpose and not find ourselves struggling with Him.

Beware of Tricksters

Joshua kept advancing and kept overcoming. As long as you keep going, you will keep gaining ground. As God is giving you victories in life and ministry, beware of tricksters. The bigger your ministry, the more susceptible you are to tricksters. Jesus had enough discernment to tell the multitude that came to Him in John 6:26: "You seek Me, not because you saw the signs, but because you ate of the loaves and were filled." There are people who come to you because they believe that they will have their physical needs met. Now, do not think that in itself is a wrong motive. No, but when you continue long in that motive you can cause damage.

You can come to God primarily because of some worldly expectations, but to remain in God with such expectations can cause you to begin to manipulate people and situations to your advantage, and that will be witchcraft. So from time to time God has to filter your motives by denying your desires for a while. Not that He has not known your response already, for He is omniscient, but for you to realize your response and amend.

When Orpah and Ruth followed Naomi to go back to Bethlehem of Judah, Naomi stopped at a point to show them that it might be futile to follow her if they had desires to marry (see Ruth 1). Orpah weighed the option of living a widowed life forever and decided she could not pay such a price and opted out. Ruth also weighed the options and decided even if she had no husband she would follow Naomi, who had shown her the ways of Jehovah, and she went on.

God said something to me—He cannot give you anything that matters too much to you. It will become an idol. But if you can let the promise die, He will give you the resurrected version, and that way idolatry will be far from your flesh.

Ruth married ultimately, but we do not know what became of Orpah. I am saying something to you, the reader—whatever you let go of for the purposes of God, He will give it back to you in His purpose. Ruth, a Gentile, became an ancestor of the Messiah. What an awesome restoration. If He did it for Ruth, He will do it for you.

The Gibeonites came to Joshua, and Joshua and all the leaders of Israel were deceived by their appearances. Things are not always the way they seem; that's why God admonishes true leadership to seek Him daily for a correct interpretation of situations. We are living in a world rife with deception, and the truth is sometimes very difficult to see except by discernment.

Perhaps the lessons of Joshua with the Gibeonites should motivate church leadership to seek God more diligently in everyday judgments of affairs. Gibeon became the only city whose inhabitants were not killed as commanded because Joshua and the leaders of Israel inadvertently made a league with them. The implications of this action were far-reaching, as Joshua later found himself in a battle to deliver the Gibeonites that was not his own, but God helped him.

> *And the men of Gibeon sent to Joshua at the camp at Gilgal, saying, "Do not forsake your servants; come up to us quickly, save us and help us, for all the kings of the Amorites who dwell in the mountains have gathered together against us"* (Joshua 10:6).

Joshua ultimately defeated all the kings of the Amorites and divided their lands by inheritance to Israel. What an example to the present leadership who sees God's heritage as their sole right and privilege. Who in their covetous practices would have assumed ownership of all the lands with their wives, children, and supporters? What the politicians in Africa do to the utter distaste of the Almighty is what the church leadership is perfecting in bits and pieces, here and there. The land is for all, the blessing for all, the prosperity for all, the spiritual development and maturity for all. The leadership that keeps the people needy is the leadership that feels they can control all the land, and the resulting constipation and suffocation will soon send them to an early grave.

THINGS EVERY LEADER MUST RUN FROM

1. Pride
2. Covetousness
3. Spiritual slothfulness and complacency
4. Lusts

These will kill any leader, no matter how anointed.

So Joshua divided the land, and there was still much more to conquer but Joshua was now old and stricken in years (see Josh. 13). One thing I can say about Joshua is that he left Israel without a properly defined leadership and so the people went apostate after he died. Although they had elders, judges, leaders, and officials, a man was needed. A man like Joshua with a vision and a mission, and that void resulted in every man doing what was right and seemly in his own eyes. See what happened to Israel in the Book of Judges.

Every time God's purpose had to be affected, a man was to be found. God is looking for men today in the Body of Christ who will stand in the gap, lead, instruct, and command the people to fully follow Him to achieve destiny. You can be that man. When I say man it is not limited to the male gender. In creation, He created the man, Adam, who gave his wife the name Eve and called her "woman," indicating that she was a man with a womb. In Christ Jesus, there is no male, no female, no freeman, no slave. We are all equal.

Can you be a Joshua for your generation? He started as a servant, and the servants are the greatest in the Kingdom. The truth is most people start with servant hearts but end up as oppressors like Saul. It is your choice and responsibility what you end up with in life.

God is looking for a people who will cooperate with His Spirit to finish His work on the earth.

Points to Ponder

1. Have a warrior mentality and the heart of a servant.
2. Never waste time reminiscing about the past; it can never be changed.
3. Be a diligent and disciplined leader so you can command the people.
4. It is time to cross the Jordan—death to self and selfish ambitions. Therefore, a second circumcision is necessary and not optional for the present Church.

CHAPTER 9

Lessons for the Twenty-first Century Church

Lessons for the Twenty-first Century Church

Having seen the patterns in the Old Testament saints, one can draw valuable conclusions for how the present Church can live above this present age and its attendant problems and temptations.

It is important to note that the God of old is the same God today. His plans and purposes have not changed regardless of the time in history. He lives in eternity but uses people in time to execute His counsels on the earth.

Generations may come and go, but He remains forever and His values do not change. On account of these facts, this present Church must avoid the pitfalls of the Church in the wilderness and align accurately with God for their generation.

This generation, to my mind and with prophetic insight, is the final generation that shall declare the name of the Lord and His righteous deeds before Christ returns to the earth.

> *A posterity shall serve Him. It will be recounted of the Lord to the next generation* (Psalm 22:30).
>
> *This is Jacob, the generation of those who seek Him, who seek Your face. Selah* (Psalm 24:6).

To fulfill this mandate, the entire concept of the church has to be redefined.

What We Must Do

Religion must be thrown out of the Church and relationships emphasized.

Leadership's functions and responsibilities must be clearly defined, and accuracy in lifestyles of leadership must not be overlooked.

The character of Christ must be the pursuit of the Church and its leadership.

The principles of God's Kingdom must be the operational principles if the Church hopes to occupy the fullness of her measure. The day when the Church lives like the world and hopes to rule the earth is over.

The Church must see herself as the catalyst that will bring about the necessary changes needed in the physiology and anatomy of the earth and its systems, therefore maintaining a non-conformist attitude. This is not an attitude of lawlessness, but that of strict adherence to the principles of God even in the face of persecution.

We can no longer maintain the status quo and wish for a sweet and better by and by. Our mindset must be that of pilgrims who have an urgent assignment to execute in their land of pilgrimage.

The pursuits of purpose must overwhelm the pursuits for things and fame. Nothing should be more urgent than the King's matter. Haste is required.

Capacity-building must precede cathedral-building.

Teaching priests must emerge and a teachable spirit return to the Church.

The spirit of this age—which is the spirit that wants people to heap up teachers who will tell them what they want to hear—must be attacked and dismissed from the Church.

Disciples must be filtered out from the multitudes, and the mixed multitude's cravings silenced. It was the mixed multitudes, who followed Israel out of Egypt, which began to cry for the cucumber and garlic of Egypt.

> *Now the mixed multitude who were among them yielded to intense craving; so the children of Israel also wept again and said: "Who will give us meat to eat? We remember the fish which we ate freely in Egypt, the cucumbers, the melons, the leeks, the onions, and the garlic; but now our whole being is dried up; there is nothing at all except this manna before our eyes!"* (Numbers 11:4-6)

The leadership should learn to remove pacifiers from the spiritual babies and let them cry their hearts out. Some will learn and some will not. The things that will affect the kingdoms of this world and turn them to Christ can never be achieved by spiritual babies. Spiritual growth is the only way to self-sustenance. If the Church can barely sustain herself, what hope is there for the world?

Principalities and powers must be confronted and weakened in their attempt to cripple the Church. Violence and force is the only language to employ.

> *And from the days of John the Baptist until now the kingdom of heaven suffers violence, and the violent take it by force* (Matthew 11:12).

There is a coming glory, and God is looking for human vessels to pour into. This is that day that all the prophets spoke about. We are living in a time when every prophecy will be fulfilled, and so there is a higher demand on the Church to be accountable and responsible.

The church that runs from responsibility is never going to be a part of this coming glory. Like the sons of Issachar of old, this is the time to know what Israel ought to do and take responsibility.

Of the sons of Issachar who had understanding of the times, to know what Israel ought to do, their chiefs were two hundred; and all their brethren were at their command (1 Chronicles 12:32).

The sons of God must emerge so as to deliver this earth from decay, bondage, and corruption. The heavens have retained Christ up till now, and the power to bring Him back is with the Church. Let us arise and fulfill our destiny and recover all that humankind lost in Eden.

The price has been paid already by Christ Himself; let's finish the commission even as we have received the mandate.

The time is now.

Epilogue

As I write this book, I have not exempted myself from the personal responsibilities of dealing with my own shortcomings and flaws. I am still struggling with some of the issues I have personally seen as the problems of the Church. I work daily to ensure that after preaching to others I will not be a castaway. We must all arrive at the measure of the fullness of the stature of Christ. It is a journey.

There are days I wake up not wanting to do the things I know are right. There is a war between the flesh and the spirit, and it is becoming increasingly difficult to obey God. But we are not alone in this fight; Jesus went through the same struggles. The Bible said He was tempted in every way as we are, and yet He was without sin (see Heb. 4:15).

This is the confidence we have—that when we make a determination to obey God in the midst of compromise and temptations, He will always provide a way of escape. As long as we remain in this physical body, there will always arise moments of striving to do the will of God.

The Scripture says, "His commandments are not grievous," (see 1 John 5:3), in other words, "I have given you all it takes to do My will."

The Holy Spirit has been given to the believer to enable us do the things that our natural strength cannot do, so we will really be without excuse. Our relationship with the Holy Spirit is key to our pleasing God. Without a functional and intimate relationship with the Spirit of God, we as believers of the twenty-first century are doomed to a life devoid of power to succeed.

Sometimes, as I look deeply into the purposes of God on the earth, I begin to fully comprehend why it is becoming more and more difficult to live an uncompromised life now. Gross darkness has indeed covered the earth, and God is fixing to cause His light to shine brightly as His people arise. He wants to make a distinction between His people and the world so as to attract the world to Himself, without which the world will perish.

The powers of darkness are putting intense pressure on the earth and its systems so as to delay or even abort the plans of God, but God forbid that the Church will look on in apathy and complacency. There is a cry from Heaven for the sons of God to arise, and this book has been about the making of those sons. Regardless of where we are on the planet or what our professions are, our primary obligation as believers is to make the world see Jesus through us, and in so doing deliver the earth and the people from demonic onslaughts.

We can all make up our minds, like the Hebrew boys in Babylon, not to defile ourselves with Babylonian dishes. Yes, our faith will be tried, but God will be glorified.

I am part of this process, and I urge you to be part of it as well. God is counting on us. We cannot afford to fail.

About Grace Emerald Udokang

Pastor Grace is a true daughter of Zion. She is uncompromising in her pursuit of God's truth and purpose handed to her as a vision.

Pastor Grace is the senior pastor and set person of the Green Pastures Christian Centre, a church-based ministry dedicated to the building of capacity of believers for the edifying of the Body of Christ in preparation for the return of the Messiah.

She is a teacher of the Word with great prophetic grace. She is the CEO of Green Pastures Crèche and executive producer of the television talk show *Green Pastures*. She has ministered across many nations in Africa with the mandate to wake up the Church in Africa to its responsibility to the nations of the earth before Christ returns.

She is married to Engr. Kufre Udokang, a mechanical engineer and partner in Christ. In addition to her four children—Ann, Truth, Andrew, and Divine—she has taken under her care many children who would otherwise have been destitute. She is also an unofficial mum to two sons—Darlyn-Moore and Stephen. She has a degree in linguistics.

Contact the Author

If you would like to contact the author, please write to:

gpccentre@yahoo.com

or visit:

www.gpchristiancentre.org

A new, exciting title from
DESTINY IMAGE™ EUROPE

YOU CAN CHANGE THE WORLD
Keys to Stepping Into Your Destiny
by CLAUDIA WINTOCH

You Can Change the World is a call to action for believers to move out of what is familiar and into the world to make a positive Kingdom difference. Now is the time to fulfill your God-given destiny and purpose by looking beyond where you live, work, and worship and into the world as God sees it.

With an international setting including Austria, England, Africa, Canada, and the United States, the author uses her own journey of pursuing God's will for her life to portray the struggles and victories that are part of living totally for Him.

Get ready to start your journey and to become the one the Lord can use to change the world.

ISBN: 978-88-96727-22-5

Order now from Destiny Image Europe
Telephone: +39 085 4716623 +39 085 8670146 • Fax +39 085 9090113
Email: orders@eurodestinyimage.com
Internet: www.eurodestinyimage.com

A new, exciting title from DESTINY IMAGE™ EUROPE

BUSINESS IN GOD
Erase the line between God's work and man's work
by BRYAN WATERS

Business in God discusses in a refreshingly simple way that even though you may be in a career or involved in daily activities that seem "non-spiritual," you can still be, and should be, on course to fulfill your God-given destiny.

Author and entrepreneur Bryan Waters shares how you can "prosper in all things" and how to apply the revelation to your daily life in practical ways. You will learn life-changing concepts including: "Spiritual Momentum," "Discipline that Leads to Freedom," and "You, Work, the Church, and the Marketplace."

Business in God proves that written on the core of every Christian's destiny is success, prosperity, good health, and sanctification—leading to transformation into the likeness of Christ. Step into your future today with confidence!

ISBN: 978-88-96727-24-9

Order now from Destiny Image Europe
Telephone: +39 085 4716623 +39 085 8670146 • Fax +39 085 9090113
Email: orders@eurodestinyimage.com

Internet: www.eurodestinyimage.com

Additional copies of this book and other book titles from DESTINY IMAGE™ EUROPE are available at your local bookstore.

We are adding new titles every month!

To view our complete catalog online, visit us at:
www.eurodestinyimage.com

Send a request for a catalog to:

Via della Scafa, 29/14
65013 Città Sant'Angelo (Pe), ITALY
Tel. +39 085 4716623 • +39 085 8670146
Fax +39 085 9090113
info@eurodestinyimage.com

"Changing the world, one book at a time."

Are you an author?

Do you have a "today" God-given message?

CONTACT US

We will be happy to review your manuscript for the possibility of publication:

publisher@eurodestinyimage.com
http://www.eurodestinyimage.com/pages/AuthorsAppForm.htm